"*In* God's Secret Listener *John Butterworth relays thrilling true stories of how God is working [illegible]lbania, basing his narrative around Bert[illegible] an A[illegible] [illegible]t Je[illegible] radio broadcast. The stories [illegible] on the radio, how missionaries were called to Albania, and [illegible] was converted and became pastor of a church.*

"There are lessons to learn here. We see that prayer is key to making things happen. Although few had heard of Albania at the time, people were praying for the country and for opportunities to take the gospel there even under the harsh regime of Enver Hoxha.

"We see that perseverance in preaching the Word is essential. Sali Rahmani recorded radio shows about God for Albania for eighteen years before receiving a letter from someone in Albania who had been listening to the programmes.

"Finally, we are reminded that there are corners of the world that we do not know about even though the world is 'shrinking'. Missionaries are needed to preach the gospel in those places, and this book reveals just how much spiritual hunger there can be in those who have never heard."

– **Rico Tice,** Associate Minister at All Souls Church, Langham Place, London

"John Butterworth's inspirational story of Berti Dosti describes the way that God is at work in the world today. In 1967 Enver Hoxha, the Communist leader of Albania, 'abolished God'. Some years later Hoxha thought he had succeeded in wiping religion out of his nation. Yet, despite all the efforts of the Communist regime, God did not forsake Albania. At great personal risk Berti responded to God's call. He not only became a Christian but also shared his faith. The results of his commitment and obedience are evident today in Albania.

"This extraordinary story is a powerful testimony to the way

that human beings need to worship. The God-implanted impulse to worship, found in every human heart, does not change whether it is confronted by militant atheism in Albania or, as in the case of much of the West, by materialism. Butterworth's account of Berti Dosti's life will inspire Christians around the world to share their faith confidently in word and deed."

– **The Rt Revd Dr Alan Smith,** Bishop of St Albans

"When we read books about how God changes people's lives, we tend to think this is something that can only happen to exceptional individuals – not to people like us. Yet the message of the Bible is that it is precisely those who feel hopelessly ill-equipped and unqualified whom God calls to bring about his purposes. Think of Moses – an ex-murderer who'd become a migrant worker – or Gideon, or Jeremiah, or the Virgin Mary, all of whom felt utterly terrified and inadequate when God's call came to them. Why does God call people who feel – and often are – poorly equipped for what he wants of them? Because then they are more likely to trust him, rather than rely on themselves.

"John Butterworth's wonderful story about the life of the Albanian army officer Berti Dosti, and his journey to Christian faith, shows us that what was true in Biblical times is just as true today. God calls people from every possible background, including (in Berti's case) an army officer in the most repressive and atheistic state in Europe, and changes their lives forever. The story of what happened to Berti is as enthralling as any spy thriller. And it leaves the reader asking him or herself: if God can call people like this, might he be calling me too? What might I have to change or give up if I want to respond to him? What amazing experiences might I miss out on if I refuse his call?

"Do read this book – and ask God to show you what his plans are for your life."

– **Gordon Mursell,** former Bishop of Stafford

ALBANIA

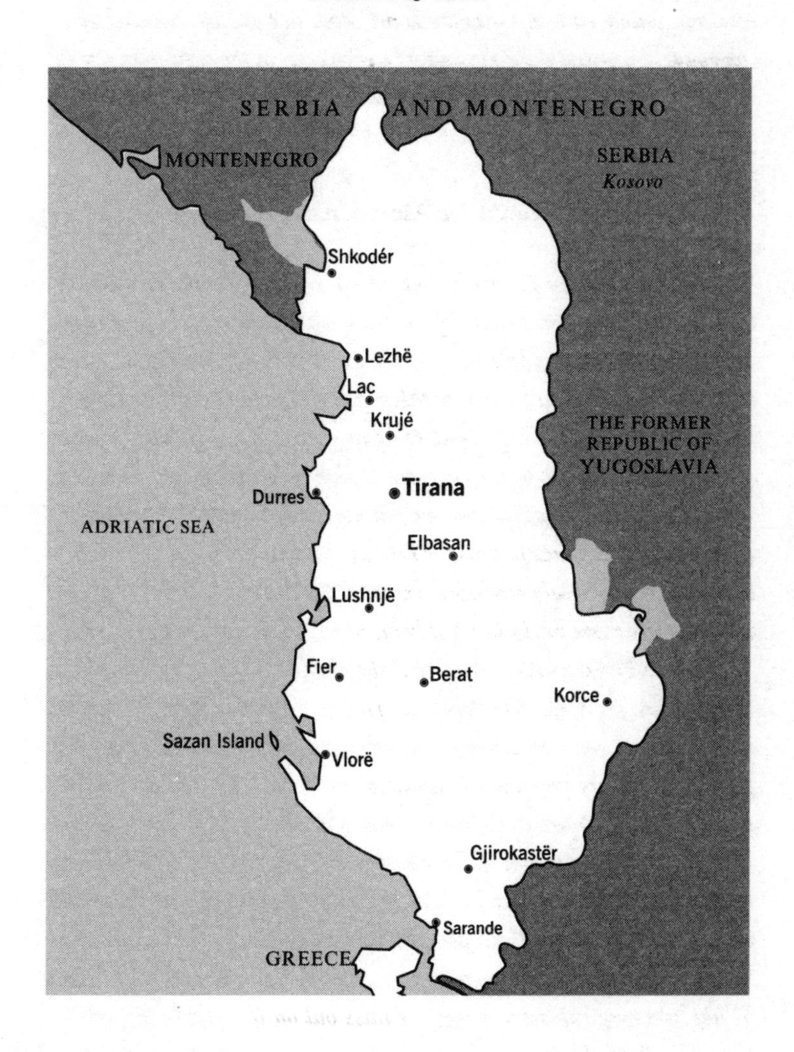
SERBIA AND MONTENEGRO
MONTENEGRO
SERBIA
Kosovo
Shkodér
Lezhë
Lac
Krujé
THE FORMER
REPUBLIC OF
YUGOSLAVIA
Durres
Tirana
ADRIATIC SEA
Elbasan
Lushnjë
Fier
Berat
Korce
Sazan Island
Vlorë
Gjirokastër
Sarande
GREECE

GOD'S SECRET LISTENER

JOHN BUTTERWORTH

MONARCH
BOOKS
Oxford, UK, & Grand Rapids, Michigan, USA

First published in the UK in 2010 by Monarch Books
(a publishing imprint of Lion Hudson plc)
Wilkinson House, Jordan Hill Road, Oxford OX2 8DR, England
Tel: +44 (0)1865 302750 Fax: +44 (0)1865 302757
Email: monarch@lionhudson.com
www.lionhudson.com

ISBN 978 1 85424 991 3

Distributed by:
UK: Marston Book Services, PO Box 269, Abingdon, Oxon, OX14 4YN
USA: Kregel Publications, PO Box 2607, Grand Rapids, Michigan 49501

The text paper used in this book has been made from wood independently certified as having come from sustainable forests.

British Library Cataloguing Data
A catalogue record for this book is available from the British Library.

Printed and bound in the UK by Cox & Wyman Ltd.

Dedication

To all those who helped me on my journey of faith, and to all those Albanian Christians who suffered under Enver Hoxha.

About the author:

John Butterworth has been a newspaper editor for 25 years editing weekly papers in Leek, Bromsgrove and Shrewsbury. In May 2008 he was awarded the MBE for services to journalism and charity after his newspapers raised more than £5m for local causes. John has also been a Reader in the Church of England since 1994.

By the same author:

Bruce's Baby (published by Henry E. Walter Ltd)
Cults and New Faiths (published by Lion)
Too Old at 40? (published privately)

CONTENTS

PREFACE

For a long time Albania lurked just within my radar. Initially I was no more than inquisitive about a nation that had banned religion and any semblance of western influence and values.

Then Albania gradually moved more to the centre of my attention.

First because I found myself interviewing a young missionary who'd visited, as a tourist, to see how things were. She'd returned with details of an almost undocumented reign of terror that had set out to eradicate all places of worship and those that would wish to use them. She also told of her divine encounters with several maintaining their faith in secret and against all odds.

Then, for several years, I led Christian groups at a holiday centre in Corfu, directly opposite Albania. Here I'd led special prayer times looking across the sea between the two – thanking God for what we were sure he'd be doing by his Spirit there and asking for a day of freedom to come.

Our prayers were a mere fraction of those prayed both within Albania and round the world. And God did what God does. He answered and freedom came. Over the following months I heard first hand accounts from those who were now sharing God's love in word and action – and seeing New Testament things happen as people came to faith and a fledgling church discovered how to fly.

All the while I was convinced I knew only a fraction of what had gone on during the dark days of vicious persecution. God had been at work behind all our backs and one day it would be told. Now, this very important book draws back the curtain.

John Butterworth brings his considerable skill and experience as a journalist in order to both document and bring to life this remarkable account of how Captain Berti Dosti became Pastor Berti Dosti.

It is written with great attention to detail. And though this may focus on just one person and one story, through it you capture the even greater narrative of an amazing God who is on a mission.

The transformation that has come to Albania is nothing compared to the transformation God is bringing to lives there – as this valuable book reveals. Read, wonder, and enjoy.

Peter Meadows
Associate Director, Bible Society

FOREWORD

I can still remember the sense of excitement as my plane approached Tirana airport. The year was 1994 and the excitement was tinged with apprehension. Tirana was an airport without meaningful radar cover and the runway was notorious for being cobbled! A very bumpy landing, a long wait to be let off the plane, and then down some rickety steps into a freezing winter night.

Once I was over the physical concerns, the political, cultural, and spiritual questions filled my mind. What will life be like in this avowedly atheistic state? How will people be adapting to life now that the dictator, Enver Hoxha, is finally gone? Has the church survived, and what does its future look like?

I discovered a land trapped in a 1940s time warp – economically impoverished, politically isolated, and spiritually barren. And yet... God's people were still to be found! Small in number, lacking in leadership, and bereft of resources... but strangely peace-filled and certain of faith. It was thrilling to preach to a small group of believers on a Sunday in the Albanian capital – a wonderful demonstration of the resilience of the church under pressure, a living example of the fact that even the "gates of hell" will not prevail against the Body of Christ!

It was against the backdrop of these experiences in Albania that I read this manuscript by John Butterworth. What a pleasure to read the inspiring story of Berti Dosti – a story of transformation, hope, conversion, and mission. God is at work in individuals and nations, in Britain and in Albania... no less in the twenty-first century than in the first.

May your faith be encouraged as you read this compelling salvation story.

Stephen Gaukroger
Clarion Trust

INTRODUCTION

Most people have heard of evangelist Billy Graham. Very few have heard of Billy Sunday. Yet Billy Sunday has played probably just as important a part in Christianity as Billy Graham has. In 1924, Billy Sunday ran a Christian campaign in Charlotte, USA, out of which came the Charlotte Businessmen's Club, which invited Dr Mordecai Ham to one of its meetings. He became a Christian at one of the rallies, and ten years later the club invited Dr Ham to lead another campaign, where a sixteen-year-old became a Christian in 1934. His name was Billy Graham.

It is interesting to trace back the people you have met on your life journey and what influences they have had on you, and I would encourage every reader of this book to do that. For many people they are just meetings of coincidence, but Christians believe they are God-incidences and that God brings people into contact for a purpose, such as for a Christian project or to help someone discover Christianity. Also, it is fascinating to trace back and see how many people over many years have been involved in bringing someone to faith.

One such person is Berti Dosti, who became a Christian even though he was a captain in the Albanian army. Albania was a closed country and its leader, Enver Hoxha, proudly declared in 1967 that his nation had "abolished God" and was the world's "first atheistic state".

I first met Berti Dosti in May 2009, when I had been made redundant after thirty-seven years in journalism and was wondering what to do next. As I talked to the former Captain Dosti, and now Pastor Dosti, I was staggered by the number of people God had used all over the world, and in the most unlikely places, to help bring him to faith, and this gave me the idea for this book.

This story shows how God spoke to Berti, and tells how many people have helped him on his journey: in particular, Sali Rahmani, Stephen Bell, and Gani Smolica.

For many people today Albania, or *Shqipëria* as it is in Albanian, translated as "the Land of the Eagle", is a forgotten country, and few people would be able to place it on a world map. The only time in the last twenty years or so when people in the UK briefly took notice of it was when England drew Albania in the same section of the 1990 World Cup qualifying competition. The English team were so suspicious about this unknown country that when they played the away game they brought their own food and their own chef, and flew home immediately after the game in March 1989 so they didn't have to stay in an Albanian hotel. If by any chance it has slipped your mind, Bryan Robson and John Barnes scored the goals as England won 2–0.

However, Albania, which is just north of Greece and across the Adriatic from Italy, is waking up after more than forty years of living under what was probably Europe's cruellest and severest totalitarian regime. The country, which has a surprising Christian heritage, has a fascinating story to tell about its own journey. It has gone from a dictatorship to a democracy, from a badly-resourced military force to a member of NATO, and from an isolated state without a friend in the world to an applicant for membership of the European Union.

This book is the journey of how Captain Berti Dosti became Pastor Berti Dosti against a backdrop of a radically changing country that is rejoining the world family.

I am indebted to many, many people, on my own life journey and for their help with this book. I would like to thank Richard Tiplady, former British director of the European Christian Mission (ECM), who sent me to Albania and started me on this fascinating project. Thanks to all at ECM, and in particular Stephen Bell and Pip Thompson, for their patience and help with my research. I am also grateful to all at Trans World Radio, especially British director Russell Farnworth, and to Tony Collins, publisher of Monarch Books at Lion Hudson plc, for all their encouragement and support.

The book would not have happened without the help of Berti and Tatjana Dosti and translator Alma Syla, who have all become close friends. It is amazing to think that if I, as a journalist and Christian, had met Captain Berti some years ago in Albania he would probably have arrested me. Berti and Tatjana have welcomed me into their home, patiently answering my probing questions. They have been very honest about their lives and talked about what must have been difficult subjects for them. Although their English is good, they felt more confident with Alma, an English teacher, interpreting. To be fluent in what are probably two of Europe's most difficult languages is no mean achievement, especially as Alma didn't learn English until her early twenties and mostly taught herself.

I am also extremely grateful to my journalist colleague and sister-in-law Jackie Gregory, who cast a careful sub-editor's eye over the manuscript and picked up many mistakes I had missed.

Finally, my eternal thanks to someone who inspired me to write the book, who gave me many constructive comments and ideas, and who has been my best friend and closest companion on my own life's journey – my wife Jan.

Chapter 1

IF YOU WANT TO FIND OUT MORE ABOUT GOD, WE WILL MEET AGAIN TOMORROW

Berti Dosti faced a terrible but intriguing dilemma. He was an Albanian army captain and his job as a radio specialist was to listen into the world's airwaves during the 1980s, because his country feared they were about to be invaded by the West. He was in the middle of a 24-hour shift and he was getting tired and bored, as he had had to do more than his fair share of duties recently. As he idly twiddled the radio dials, he heard a voice saying, "If you want to find out more about God, we will meet again tomorrow."

Like all Albanians, 32-year-old Berti had been told God didn't exist and that anyone caught showing an interest in religion could expect a huge punishment to be imposed not only on him, but also on his family, his children and even his grandchildren. Still something intrigued Berti; something stirred deep inside him. But how could he dare take up that invitation, putting his whole family at risk? And anyway, how could he listen in secretly when one in two Albanian army personnel were reckoned to be government spies?

For five nights a week Trans World Radio, a Christian

station in Monte Carlo, beamed a fifteen-minute programme in Albanian on 1467 kilohertz (kHz), 600 miles over Italy and across the Adriatic into this secretive and unknown country. Although these two places were only a few hundred miles apart and both were in Europe, there the similarity ended – in reality they were worlds apart.

Monte Carlo was a luxury resort, a tax exile and home of millionaires in the principality of Monaco, in the south-eastern Mediterranean corner of France. It wanted to attract visitors, preferably the super-rich, whether they were film stars on location, gamblers at its casino, or Formula 1 stars racing in the Monaco Grand Prix.

On the other hand, Albania, just above Greece and opposite the heel of Italy, had a slightly different tourism policy – no visitors welcome under any circumstances. The nearest any foreigner from the West was likely to get to visiting Albania in the 1970s and 80s was if a sun-worshipper on the nearby Greek island of Corfu in a boat or an inflatable dinghy happened to stray into Albanian waters. The watching Albanian military would quickly show them the error of their ways and force them into an about-turn back to the island's beaches.

After taking power in 1944, Enver Hoxha had turned Albania into the world's most isolated country, ruling it with Stalinist tyranny and fear. He was determined to wipe out religion, proudly declaring in 1967 that Albania was the "first atheist country in the world". Hoxha, repeating a phrase taken from the nineteenth-century nationalist leader Pashko Vasa, said, "There is no religion in Albania, except being an Albanian."

With a ruthless campaign, the fanatical despot waged war on religion just as he had done against the Fascist Italian and German occupiers during the Second World War. He destroyed churches or converted them into post offices, schools, weapon depots, cafés, barns, storehouses, or museums. The cathedral at Shkodra was even turned into a volleyball court, and in 1972 a museum of atheism was opened in that city. For the last twenty-three years of his Communist rule there was not a single functioning church in the country. All 2,169 religious establishments, which included mosques, 268 Roman Catholic churches, and buildings of other denominations and other faiths, were closed. Of the country's 1,600 Orthodox churches, monasteries, and cultural centres in 1967, fewer than eighty were still standing when Communism ended in 1991.[1]

Many Orthodox priests and evangelical Christians were sent to prison, tortured, and then executed by firing squad. During Hoxha's reign of terror, 335 Orthodox priests died by execution, or from mistreatment, untreated illnesses, and exhaustion. By the time it finished, only twenty-two Orthodox priests were still alive. Religious institutions were forbidden to have any connections or headquarters outside Albania, so the Roman Catholic Church had to cut its links with Rome and was designated instead as the Independent Catholic Church of Albania.

The constitution banned all "fascist, religious, warmongerish, anti-socialist activity and propaganda". Prison sentences of between three and ten years were imposed for "religious propaganda" and for the production, distribution, or storage of religious literature. Another decree targeted Christian names. Any citizen whose name did not conform to "the political, ideological or moral standards of the state" was required to change it. To help parents, the government published lists with pagan names to choose from, including newly-created names such as Marenglen (a combination of Marx, Engels, and Lenin). A new girl's name, Enveriada, was invented in honour of Enver

Hoxha, while his nicknames of Shpati and Tarasi also became accepted names for children.

Despite this, Albanians were proud of their history and knew they had a rich religious heritage. In the Bible, in Romans 15:19, the Apostle Paul states, "So from Jerusalem all the way round to Illyricum, I have fully proclaimed the gospel of Christ." Illyricum was the Roman province that covered part of present-day Albania, the Dalmatian coast, Kosovo, Bosnia and Herzegovina, and Montenegro, with the River Sava forming the northern border.

The Catholic historian Daniele Farlati stated that Paul came to Dyrrachium, the modern port of Durres, and many Albanians believe it, although there is no proof. However, the biblical historian F. F. Bruce points out that in Acts 20 Paul travelled through Greece, and it was likely that he travelled along the Egnatian Way, which continued to Thessalonica and on to Constantinople (modern Istanbul). Dyrrachium was the western end of that great Roman road.[2] By AD 59, Dyrrachium had its first Christian bishop and up to seventy Christian families were living there.

Ironically, while Hoxha was trying to tell the world there were no Christians and no religion in Albania, one of the most famous Christians in the world at that time was Albanian-born Mother Teresa, who became a Catholic nun and whose work with the poor in Calcutta, India, attracted world headlines.

Meanwhile, Berti had been taught Albanian history at school without reference to the country's religious heritage. This made his current dilemma about a sudden interest in God much more difficult. He wanted to listen to the following night's Trans World Radio broadcast without anyone knowing. However, he knew that if he were caught he could be stripped of his uniform, thrown out of the army, and sent to jail. That would bring disgrace on his family. His father and his brother had both been soldiers – what would they think of his "treason"? His Communist Party biography, or record of achievements, would mean nothing, and he probably would never work again, or he would be sent away to a remote part of Albania. His wife and children would suffer, their party biography would be blemished, and his children and grandchildren would not be allowed to go to university and would lose all the privileges that being a good member of the Party brought. Finally, it would bring an inglorious end to a brilliant military career for Captain Dosti, who was now in charge of his military base and who had already, at twenty-nine years of age, been awarded the third highest military medal in Albania, which made him one of the youngest ever winners of the Urdhëri i Shërbimit Ushtarak të Klasit III.

As Berti pondered all this, he suddenly realized how he could listen in to that Trans World Radio programme – and no one would know.

Chapter 2

A PIONEERING SPIRIT

Being born into an army family was not easy for Berti, who lived in six different homes across Albania in the first ten years of his life. What made it more difficult for him was that his parents, Shefit and Antoneta, divorced when he was just three years old. He and his older brother, six-year-old Iliri, were separated and never lived under the same roof again. Berti stayed with his father, an army officer, while Iliri went to live with an uncle, and neither of them saw their mother again for thirty years.

Berti was born on 11 April 1957, in Korçë, the regional capital of south-east Albania and not far from the Greek border. He has few memories of his early years there, though he was to return to Korçë later in life on a very poignant mission.

Although it is a bit out on a limb, this attractive town with interesting Ottoman buildings has played an important part in the country's rich religious and historical heritage. One of its most famous residents was Gjerasim Qiriazi, a nineteenth-century evangelical preacher and a pioneering educationalist who, with his sister, set up a school for girls in Korçë. In 1882 he started the Evangelical Brotherhood of Albania, to unite people to work for the good of the nation.

Another famous resident was the Albanian dictator Enver Hoxha. Although born in Gjirokastra on 16 October 1908, the son of a cloth merchant, he moved to the French Lycée in Korçë, where he studied French, history, literature, philosophy and the Communist manifesto. Ironically, with a state scholarship given by the Albanian Queen Mother, he went to study biology at the University of Montpellier in France before moving to Paris, where he joined the French Communist Party. In 1936 he returned to Korçë to teach and helped found an underground Communist organization. Following the 1939 Italian invasion, he was dismissed as a teacher for refusing to join the Albanian Fascist Party. He then opened a tobacconist's shop, called Flora, in Tirana, where a small group of Communists began to gather, until the government closed it down.[1]

After the divorce, Berti moved with his father from Korçë to Kamëz, near Tirana, where Shefit's brother lived. They stayed there for three years, with the family looking after Berti whenever Shefit was working. At the end of this period, however, Shefit remarried. Six-year-old Berti took a dim view of this, as did the military authorities. Even in Stalinist Albania, divorce was frowned upon. Within a few weeks, the family were sent to Sazan Island. This island, measuring just four kilometres by five kilometres, lies in the Bay of Vlorë off the south-western corner of Albania. It has always been of strategic importance, occupied by the Italians before the First World War, an important Soviet base in the 1950s, and housing United States military advisers to the Albanian Government in the 1990s. It was the one place a soldier never wanted to go to. Officers would threaten recruits: "If you don't behave, you will be posted to Sazan Island."

Berti remembers the island, about forty-five minutes' boat ride from Vlorë, as a huge forest with a field in the middle where there was a military base and a small school for officers' children. For a young boy growing up, there were plenty of places to explore. But as no one could leave this strategic island, which would probably have borne the full force of any first assault if the West had ever attacked Albania, the novelty soon wore off.

Within two years, the grateful Dosti family were packing again to drive up the Albanian coast to the north-west of the country, almost to the Montenegro border, where the town of Shëngjin awaited, with its long sandy beach and a history of political intrigue. Early in the twentieth century it was the centre for international tension involving the Russians, the Austrians, the Serbs, the Montenegrins, the Yugoslavs and the British. Sir Harry Eyres, whose whitewashed house is still on the waterfront at Shëngjin, was a former Lloyd's shipping agent who became a spy in the 1920s and later became the first British diplomat to be resident in Albania.[2]

Berti lived there for less than a year in a condominium on the beach, where he enjoyed beachcombing for seashells and his "treasure" – plastic bottles that were washed up on the beach. In the early 1960s, plastic bottles were rare in Albania, and Berti enjoyed putting them on a shelf by his bed – with the ultimate find being a plastic Coca Cola bottle.

It wasn't long before Berti and family were off again in an army lorry and heading for nearby Lezha, one of the most famous towns in Albania. It was where people came to visit the tomb of their national hero, Gjergjj Kastrioti Skenderbeu. Born in 1405, Skenderbeu was taken hostage by the Turks with his three brothers in 1423, and when their father, Gjon, died, three of the brothers were poisoned. Gjergjj was the only one who survived. He joined the Ottoman Turks' army and did so well that he was hailed "Chief of the League of the Albanian People" and was given the name Skenderbeu, after Alexander the Great. He then reconverted to Christianity, changed sides and was named "Champion of Christendom" by Pope Nicholas V for his battle with the Turkish invaders. He died in 1468 of fever and was buried in Lezha on 17 January. However, the Turks had their revenge. When they took the town at the end of the fifteenth century they dug up his body in St Nicholas' Church, dismembered it and made charms out of his bones. Today a bronze bust of Skenderbeu stands on the nave floor, with replicas of a sword and a helmet.[3]

By now, Berti was used to moving school and found it easy to make new friends, partly because he much preferred to be out exploring rather than stay at home. He was very intelligent and could soon adapt, as the syllabus was the same at all primary schools – writing, reading, a little Albanian history and geography, plus the most important subject, education. This was studying what Enver Hoxha said and how everyone in Albania should behave. To remind them of their allegiance, all pupils had to gather outside their school every day and a teacher would ask them, "Pupils and students at war, for the sake of the Party and the nation, are you ready?" To which they would reply in unison: "Always ready."

Just eighteen months later, Berti was again putting his worldly possessions and treasures into an army van, as the family headed a few miles south to the industrial town of Laç – and two life-changing events.

The most important occasion for Berti and all young Albanians was when they reached the age of nine and became Pioneers. Berti remembers his own special Pioneers' day, when the whole class was taken to the Place of the Heroes graveyard and had to line up in front of the Albanian flag. This flag, with a black double-headed eagle on a dark red background, is one of the most ancient in Europe and very emotive to the Albanian people, as it was Skenderbeu's flag when he fought for his country's independence.

When the National Assembly of Vlorë proclaimed Albanian independence on 28 November 1912, it approved the flag as a symbol of the Albanian nation. The double-headed eagle shows their dual Christian heritage through the Western Catholic tradition and the Orthodox East. The horizontal open-winged eagle also symbolizes that the highland Albanians will not submit to foreign conquest. When the Communists took control after the Second World War they added a yellow, five-pointed star to the flag, but this was removed after independence in 1990.

The director and vice-director of the school asked the youngsters to swear allegiance before the flag. They would reply by promising "to give our lives, our last drop of blood for the Party". Each pupil was presented with a triangular red scarf symbolizing the blood of the heroes who had given their lives fighting the enemy. It was considered a holy scarf, which they were expected to wear all the time. If they didn't, they were insulting the national heroes and their sacrifice.

Berti said that at an early age you were taught to be careful what you thought and what you said. If you ever misbehaved, you were asked, "Is this the behaviour our Party wants? Do you want to oppose the Party? Do you not want to honour the heroes?" The ultimate discipline at every school was the threat to take away the scarf. If a young child went around without their scarf, it was obvious they had done wrong and so were open to persecution and ridicule.

Other than the Pioneer ceremony, Berti remembers little of Laç, as every year he was sent all the way across Albania to spend the summer with his stepmother's family at Melcan, a small farming community near Korçë. Berti thoroughly enjoyed his holidays there, playing in the fields with his stepmother's four cousins and living a simple, rural life looking after their cows and sheep – from the age of seven, all the village children went to the local primary school six days a week and then helped on the land on Sundays.

All young Albanian children had divided loyalties regarding their mothers. From an early age, they were taught: "I have two mothers. The first and the greatest one is the Mother Party, and then my mother." Although Berti went to his stepmother's family for a number of holidays, he was never allowed to go back to the nearby town of his birth – his father did not want him to have any contact with his natural mother, Antoneta. Ironically, the only time he did go to Korçë was when his stepmother's father took him for a treat on his horse to the town market. Suddenly, he went white and quickly turned the horse in the other direction, and Berti saw a face in the crowd. To this day, he is convinced that was his real mother.

After the summer break, Berti would take the long journey across Albania by bus back to his father and stepmother in Laç and return to his own school. He didn't realize it then, but the second oldest of his stepmother's nieces, Tatjana, was to play an important role in his life – and when later in life he returned to Laç, from the south of Albania, it was in much more frightening circumstances.

Chapter 3

WE'RE IN THE ARMY NOW

After ten years of moving around, Berti at last had some stability in his life when at the end of December 1967 he, his father, his stepmother, and her daughter Alma were transferred to Lushnjë, a medium-sized lowland industrial town. It would be home for Berti for the next forty years or more, and it was the start of a lifelong friendship with a neighbour's boy, Ladi, who would keep cropping up throughout Berti's life when help was most needed. The nine-year-old was a year younger than Berti, but they soon became close friends, especially as Ladi had a large house with a big garden, ideal for football and hide-and-seek. They didn't go to the same school, but as soon as Berti returned home, he dashed out again to play in Ladi's garden. He was in their house so often that he became almost part of the family of Liri and her husband Leksi, who was a tailor. "Berti was a very quiet lad," recalled Ladi's mother, Liri, "but he was always so well behaved."

Berti and Ladi lived close to the town's most famous and historic house, where the Congress of Lushnjë was held. It was there in 1920 that Muslim, Catholic and Orthodox members took a historic vote for total national independence, the first town in Albania to do so. In 1913, the London Conference of Ambassadors had declared Albania to be an independent sovereign state. However, a large part of northern and western Albania was given to Serbia, while Greece received the large southern region of Çamëria, leaving more than half the Albanian population living outside the borders of the new state. This was a problem that would resurface more than seventy-five years later with the Kosovo war.

When, in April 1915, a secret treaty was made in London to partition most of the remainder of Albania between Greece and Italy, the Albanians sent representatives to the 1919 Paris Peace Conference to argue for the restoration of their nation. A year later, the Congress of Lushnjë was set up. The 1921 Conference of Ambassadors in Paris again recognized Albania as an independent sovereign state, and three years later a young tribal leader, Ahmet Zogu, returned from exile in Yugoslavia to lead the country and was later crowned King Zog.[1]

In Lushnjë, Berti finished his primary school education and started his four years at secondary school, where he became interested in electronics and radios. Being the son of an Albanian army officer, he had a privileged upbringing, as the military had a higher than average salary and better housing than many. Berti lived in a two-bedroom house with a kitchen, good furniture, a TV (albeit with Albanian programmes only), and a fridge. As an officer, his father had some perks, including uniform, boots and shoes, and some free groceries.

Berti was fortunate: many thousands of Albanians had a much tougher time.

Typical of those was Alma Syla, who was born in Lushnjë in 1972, and whom Berti was later to employ as an English teacher at his school. Alma and her two brothers were born to Mustafa and Ervehe, who had little education, no profession and who worked for the government in the collective farming fields, earning very little money. They lived in a three-roomed house, consisting of a bedroom, a kitchen and a tiny bathroom. One of Alma's brothers slept in the bedroom with his parents, while she and her other brother slept in the kitchen. The family couldn't afford to buy beds, so their father made them out of spare wood and plastic strips. The only other furniture was a table, a bench, and a couple of chairs, and one cupboard. There was no tap in the kitchen: the only one was in the bathroom, along with a sink and a toilet. It was not until 1987, when Alma was fifteen, that the family could afford to buy their first TV.

Alma's parents left the family home six days a week at 6 a.m. and walked for around thirty minutes to arrive at the fields and start work at 6:45 a.m. Apart from an hour for lunch, they didn't return home until 6 p.m. The workers were allowed to eat vegetables from the fields for their lunch, and many put some in their bags to take home for their families. "The authorities realized what was going on, but they turned a blind eye," said Alma. "They knew the workers were so poor that if they didn't allow it some of them would starve to death."

When their mother returned home, she made the family their only hot meal of the day, a vegetable dish. Meat was scarce and a luxury. Alma remembers being asked one year what she would like for her birthday. She replied, "Some meat." She said there was often so little food in the house that for breakfast she had just bread with water to soften it and some sugar on top. Some days she went to school, from 7:30 until 1:30, without any breakfast. When Alma returned home she would play games in the road with her friends until her mother came back from the fields.

Although school and medical treatment were free, parents had to pay to send their children to university and for medicines.

Children were sick quite often, as many houses were built without any foundations and there were consequently problems with condensation, which did nothing for their health. Many families had to spend all their money on providing food, and Alma knew of adults who would regularly sell their own blood so they could pay for extras such as education and medicine bills. Despite all this, Alma said there were no problems between the children of the military and other children. They all wore the same clothes, but the workers had to save hard while the soldiers got them free.

Nevertheless, there were some disadvantages for army families, with Berti's father having to work away for days and weeks on end. With transport difficult and many of the bases isolated it was difficult to go anywhere, even once you had permission to leave camp. "As long as you behaved, life wasn't too bad. But if you stepped out of line life could become unbearable," said Berti. "We thought we had enough, we didn't realize there was more. We did not know what life was like in the outside world. We thought this life was normal."

Berti said that everyone, including children, was watched all the time. They were observed for how they lived and what they said. The state drew up a biography on all its citizens, and even comments by a relative or enemy could influence this. The worst thing that could happen was to be labelled an enemy of the Party, in which case you could be sent to a labour camp or forced to work on land miles away from home. In the 1960s, a family misdemeanour could mean children banned from going to school, although this was rarer in the 1970s as the Party launched a campaign against illiteracy.

After becoming a Pioneer at nine, the next stage for an

Albanian was to join the Youth Organization at fourteen, which they remained in until they were eighteen. Like all Albanian children, when Berti became a Pioneer he attended a ceremony where he was presented with a special book, with his name, age, and organization number on it. The children didn't need to wear the triangular red scarf, but to ensure each student took their role seriously, each school had its own youth organization and leader, usually one of the teachers.

However, within months Berti nearly blotted his biography for life. From the age of fourteen to eighteen, every Albanian student had to spend a month each year working in the fields, and when the harvest was due they had to work Sundays as well. That summer Berti and the rest of his school were taken to the village of Plug, a ten-minute bus ride away from Lushnjë. When they arrived there were about 800 students, and the eighty teachers divided the fields so that each pupil had three rows of corn to harvest. The adult workers moved on to other fields, and Berti and the other teenagers were left to cut the tall corn with their own hands and peel away the dried leaves.

It was hard work, the weather was warm, and Berti soon got bored with harvesting. With the corn taller than the students it was easy to hide, so Berti and two friends spent a pleasant morning chatting – until a male teacher discovered them. He lashed out at them, hitting and kicking them so much that Berti decided to leave the secondary school for good and go home.

Fortunately, his father was away with the military for a month and his stepmother didn't know what Berti was doing. The first month of the school year was spent harvesting and registering for that year's lessons. When his father did return home, it was too late for Berti to enrol for that year. There was a huge row as he accused his son of being a "bad boy", the ultimate disgrace for Albanian families. Shefit said he had let the family down, while Berti shouted back that he was bored with school and, as he was fourteen now, he wanted to leave, get a job, and learn a professional skill.

His father went to see the school, and the teacher and parent agreed that Berti should return to school the following year. In the meantime, he joined the building trade for six months – a job which he recalled was hard work, taught him much about electrics, and gave him some independence.

The following April his father persuaded him to go in the September to Durres High School, a technical academy. It meant Berti leaving Lushnjë to go to the port of Durres, an hour and a half's journey away. Although his father had to pay, the advantages were that Berti left home and, most importantly, it gave him the chance to complete a diploma as an electrical technician, which would eventually give him a career. When he left the technical college four years later, he returned to Lushnjë to work for an electrical company for a month before being tempted by the big industrial complex of Elbasan – and the prospect of better pay.

Enver Hoxha had left a lasting legacy on the whole of Albania, but the town that probably changed the most under him was Elbasan. With its narrow cobbled streets, historic buildings, and public gardens, this former Roman fortress town was one of the most pleasant and unspoilt Ottoman cities in Albania. It then underwent intensive industrial development under the Communists. The ugly modern structures and a huge "Steel of the Party" metallurgical complex outside the city, built with Chinese assistance in the 1960s and 70s, led Hoxha to call it "the second national liberation of Albania".

The complex was designed to refine ferro-chrome, nickel, and other ores, and its steel production facilities turned it into a pollution nightmare. With its chimneys, the tallest in the Balkans, belching out smoke and dangerous pollutants into the atmosphere, it soon destroyed the prosperous agricultural area. Although the complex has been cleaned up, it will take a long time before the town is restored to its original splendour. Fortunately, though, some interesting buildings have survived.

One of the most noteworthy is a yellow bungalow, 6 Rr Universitetit, the home of a widow, Peggy Hasluck, who during the Second World War was the Special Operations Executive (SOE) expert on Albania, and was responsible for briefing the British liaison officers parachuted in by the SOE to help the Albanian resistance movement. Her other claim to fame was that through her relationship with Lef Nosi she was probably the first Englishwoman to have a love affair with an Albanian clan leader.[2]

Berti didn't see much of the town: he worked eight hours a day, with Sundays off. But like all the other workers there, he did as much overtime as possible and always worked his day off, helping to put electricity lines into the new steel factory ovens. Having lived in a school dormitory, he was happy in the hostel for men. There was a hostel for women, but the two sexes were kept well apart. "It was a good place to earn money," recalled Berti, who had volunteered to go there. "It was hard work, but as most of the workers were single it didn't matter, and we enjoyed our time there."

All the equipment came from China and there were many Chinese specialists overseeing the project. Berti was there when Enver Hoxha fell out with Chairman Mao and the Chinese experts were forced to leave the country. To China's surprise, the

Albanians took on the work, quickly adapted, and ensured the plant continued without their help.

When his year's contract in Elbasan ended in June 1978, Berti returned to Lushnjë and his old electrical company. However, by the end of the year two important events had happened to him. First, his father persuaded him to join the army and second, he became engaged. As Berti's older brother Iliri had enlisted in the army, it was expected that Berti would follow in the family tradition. Only one child per family was allowed to go to university for free, so Iliri had gone to study as an officer, while Berti had to work his way up through the ranks.

Despite his laziness in the cornfield, Berti still had a good party biography. It was therefore no surprise that with his family record, his industrial experience and being a youngster who enjoyed gymnastics, he was given an interview to join the army. He passed the physical tests and the political theory, and on 1 September he reported to Tirana Military School for two years' intensive training – and no holidays. Because of his interest in radios, he was put in the communications group, with about thirty other military trainees. "Although I wasn't one of the strongest physically in the group, I made up for it because I had worked in industry and was a little older," said Berti.

His father also had a bearing on another important decision that year for Berti. Even in the 1970s and 80s, arranged marriages were the norm in Albania, although it is much less common now. His father said he had had discussions with the family and he would like Berti to consider marrying Tatjana Dervishi, his stepmother's niece. Tatjana's father, a chief accountant, was a Communist, although like his wife he had been brought up to follow Bektashi, a little-known strain of Islam, founded by a

Persian, Haji Bektas Veli, in the thirteenth century. Bektashis believe that God is the Divine Spirit of Goodness, and that he is manifest at different times through different beings, one of whom they believe was Jesus Christ.

In Albanian tradition, a younger brother had to discuss the marriage arrangements with his older brother and get his agreement before talking to his bride-to-be. In December 1979, having got his brother's consent, he told his father he would marry Tatjana, and on 2 September 1980 both families gathered to celebrate the engagement.

In the following autumn Berti and Tatjana were married in her village of Melcan on Saturday 24 October 1981. His childhood friend Ladi played a vital part in getting Berti to the ceremony on time. Ladi's father made the bridegroom's wedding suit, but the tailor was very busy, and so after making the final adjustments, there wasn't much time for Berti to catch the Lushnjë train to Korçë. An added problem was that with all the heavy rain that Saturday and puddles everywhere, Berti feared getting his new suit muddy. So Ladi carried him the 700 metres from his home to the railway station – on piggyback.

Tatjana, who married in a white wedding dress, said it was a memorable day. There were more than 100 guests in the village hall for the Saturday night event, which lasted for up to six hours and included food, drink, and dancing. There were no bridesmaids and no wedding photographs. The only wedding photograph Tatjana has of her and her new husband was taken in a studio three weeks later – in black and white.

This contrasted greatly with Tatjana's daughter Alta's wedding on 11 September 2005. Alta, who was then twenty-two, chose her own husband, 27-year-old Lenci Mene, who was born in Gjirokastër, the son of an army officer and an accountant. They met at a student camp in Sarande, and as they were both Christians, they were married in a church on a Sunday at 9 a.m. Alta wore a white dress and had three bridesmaids, and more than 100 friends and family attended the service. This was followed by a reception at 11 a.m. in a Lushnjë restaurant, to which the couple were taken by luxury car. During the reception, messages from friends all over the world were relayed onto a large screen, and enough colour wedding photographs were taken to fill a large album. Afterwards, the couple flew off for a honeymoon in Turkey. Interestingly, the only guest from Berti's side of his family at his wedding was his brother Iliri. Although his father didn't attend Berti's ceremony in Korçë, he did attend his granddaughter's wedding with Berti's stepmother.

After their wedding, Berti and Tatjana had a meal with Berti's father in Tirana while they were on the way to their new home in Lushnjë. However, the house wasn't that new to Berti. It was his family home, which the army had allowed Berti to keep when he finished his military training as his father had already moved north to the capital. But what did Tatjana think of the two contrasting marriages and having to leave the village where she had grown up? "At my own wedding," said Tatjana, "I was more worried about how the reception would go. But at Alta's wedding, I was more worried about how the ceremony would go, as we were now a Christian family."

As for her own wedding, she said everyone respected their parents' authority, particularly in the villages. "With moving from a village I knew life was good in the bigger towns, so I looked forward to it," she said.

What did she think of the two families' choice of her bridegroom?

Chapter 4

OFFICER MATERIAL

Berti didn't really want to get promotion and become an officer in the Albanian army. However, he and Tatjana had been married for two years and they now had a daughter, Alta, who was born on 28 February 1983, so money was tight. For the last two years, since leaving military school, he had been working back in Lushnjë repairing radios, mainly for the army, and he was enjoying himself. However, the salary for an army radio technician was quite low and there were no promotion prospects. In addition, his father and brother expected him to become an officer, so he agreed to apply. Even in Communist Albania, it was not what you knew, but who you knew. His father Shefit, who had a fine military record, sent a request to the high command for Berti to become an officer.

Shefit also had a story to tell. He had started his military career by volunteering as a fourteen-year-old to help the Partisans during the Second World War. Although too young to fight the Italians and Germans, he was used by the Partisans as a messenger between units and villages. When in 1941 Germany invaded Russia, and at the same time turned Albania into a puppet state, the Communist Party in Albania decided it was a just war because it was now anti-fascist. The party's main figure was Enver Hoxha, who helped set up a countrywide National Liberation Movement, which in 1943 was expanded into a National Resistance Army (nicknamed the Partisans). The Germans nearly destroyed the Partisans, driving them into the mountains. The only country to help them was Britain, which provided weapons, ammunition, and clothing. These were delivered by parachute at night, and then the messengers, including Berti's father, took them to the Partisans.

David Smiley, who worked for British Intelligence and who liaised with Albanian resistance groups, had been puzzled that his reports and requests failed to get through to the Special Operations Executive. After the war, he was again shocked when details of a secret operation to train non-Communist Albanian troops outside Albania to resist Hoxha appeared to be known to the dictator. It was only years later that he realized the infamous British spy turned traitor, Kim Philby, had been betraying British secrets over Albania.[1]

When the war ended for Albania in late 1944, young people, including Berti's father, flocked to join the army full-time. Hoxha turned the National Liberation Movement into a Communist revolution, eventually winning undisputed leadership of the Party of Labour and then of Albania. Ironically, it was British arms, not Russian or Chinese, which had helped him to power.

Because Berti was highly qualified with three diplomas, and because of his family's record, he didn't have an interview to be an officer. The next day, 6 August 1983, Berti was told to report to the Sulzotaj garrison, which was west of Lushnjë on the Adriatic coast.

At that time, Albania was continually on high military alert. It was utterly isolated, having fallen out in turn with its three allies, Yugoslavia, Russia, and China. Berti said the military were particularly worried that America, Russia, or Britain would invade. The leaders were so paranoid that if an American warship passed near the Albanian coast on its way through the Adriatic, the whole country was put on full military alert.

Hoxha also fell out with Britain, soon forgetting the help Albania had received during the war. In an episode known as the Corfu Channel Incident, which was really three early Cold War clashes, floating mines struck two British destroyers, HMS *Saumarez* and HMS *Volage*, on 22 October 1946, killing forty-four men and injuring fifty-two. The Albanians claimed the British ships had strayed into their territorial waters, but the International Court of Justice at The Hague ruled the British case was legitimate. Albania refused to pay any compensation, so Britain impounded Albanian gold reserves in the Bank of England in London, and the dispute was not resolved until 1992.[2]

Berti's job, as an expert in radios and communications, was to scan the airwaves for any hint that an enemy was approaching. He also was in charge of communications between the guns and gunners so that they could be moved to the correct position when an enemy was detected, and he was the link with the command centre in case of an attack. Finally, he oversaw all radio, telephone, and signals communications within the base, including using couriers if necessary. On top of that, every year for three months he had to teach the newly conscripted soldiers how to use radios. The rest of the time was spent planning for an invasion and considering how the Albanians should respond.

Berti said they had hours of studying maps, planning war games on a table, and thinking through every scenario. He had to help answer questions from superiors, such as, What about food?

What about transportation? If the enemy attacked point X, how would we respond? What if they attacked point Y, or even point Z? "We got bored. It was always the same thing, meetings about war game meetings; it was so unreal," recalled Berti.

However, for five days every month it did become more real as they carried out war scenarios, moving equipment around and going through the procedures with different military passwords each time. "After that," said Berti, "it was practising for the next practice." Nevertheless, these exercises did show that their Chinese and Russian radios were not very reliable. They had to keep changing frequencies in order to get a signal, and Berti knew that Italy and other foreign countries had far more sophisticated radios. Berti realized that the Albanian military wouldn't be able to hold off an enemy for long, so he ensured that when all their communications were knocked out he still had human couriers to continue any war effort.

With all these long hours of boredom, did he ever wonder if an enemy existed? "Yes, I did," said Berti, "especially as I never ever came across a foreign and dangerous signal. However, I only thought it. To doubt out loud the existence of an enemy and to worry that we might lose a war was unpatriotic and totally unthinkable." He kept these thoughts to himself during the next three years as he moved up the command structure to be in charge of the base.

With Enver Hoxha in charge, everyone in communist Albania was supposedly equal and no soldier officially had a rank – that is apart from Enver Hoxha, who was General Colonel of the Albanian army and General Commandant of the Albanian navy. Army ranks were not reinstated officially until 1990, but everyone knew what rank soldiers were, particularly when they lined up for an official photograph and the leaders were on the front row. Berti added, "We thought we were all equal, and we believed it. But what was said in Albania was different to what happened."

Chapter 5

TEARS AS ENVER HOXHA DIES

Thursday 11 April 1985 was the day Albanians and many Albania-watchers abroad will never forget. The people were shocked to be told that their leader Enver Hoxha had died aged seventy-six, especially as they had no idea that he had been ill for the previous couple of years with diabetes. His illness was a state secret; the few people who knew about it could have been sent to jail, or even put to death, had they divulged the information to anyone.

At the time, Berti was working at the Sulzotaj base, and since he was an officer he was able to live at home most of the time with his family in Lushnjë. That Thursday began as a normal day, when he left home at 5 a.m. to catch the military bus to the base. As an officer, he worked 8 a.m. to 4 p.m. six days a week and alternate Sundays, plus sleeping over at the base two or three times a week. When Berti arrived at 7:30 a.m. he noticed immediately a different atmosphere. No one spoke, there was silence everywhere, and everyone kept their heads bowed, as though they didn't want to catch anyone's eyes and have to talk.

All the officers were called immediately to the Commandant's office for a meeting. "He was very solemn, very emotional, and trying to fight back the tears," recalled Berti. The Commandant said he had received a secret coded message from the Albanian government, adding, "I have some bad news to report, but you have to keep it secret." He then told them that Enver Hoxha had died. "Everyone at the base cried: even I did," admitted Berti. "It was a case of the more a person cried the more it honoured our leader. Looking back now I laugh at how much I cried."

Half an hour later at every factory, school, office, and collective farm throughout the country, the local party secretary called the people together. By now, everyone knew something had happened, because there was sombre music on the radio, but few guessed what it was.

Alma Syla, then a thirteen-year-old pupil, was with the other students in her class, working in the fields. They had to have four lessons a week learning to grow crops. The youngsters knew something was up that Thursday morning, because their teacher had stayed in the corner of the field crying and talking to one of the supervisory teachers. However, it wasn't until 9:30 a.m. that she called the students across.

In between tears, she sobbed, "Our beloved leader, our greatest person, is no more." After announcing the news, she told the students to stop working, go home, and report to school the next day. They were encouraged to watch TV, which was showing films of Hoxha's life and many tributes being paid to the leader against a backdrop of funereal music.

"Almost every one of us cried," recalled Alma, "including myself. We were frightened; we didn't know what was going to happen next. We believed Enver Hoxha had made our country secure, a strong castle, that no one would attack. But what would we be like now without a leader?"

Back at the military base, the country was put on the highest military alert and the volunteer force was told to be ready for immediate call-up. The national leaders were worried that the army might lose its discipline, that external enemies might seize the opportunity to attack Albania, or that internal enemies might lead an uprising and overthrow the government. Berti said there were special organizations within the army and government to ensure there was no internal revolt, as many intellectuals would be glad to see the end of Hoxha's regime. "But they celebrated in silence," said Berti, "and they cried in public, because there were so many spies watching them to see their reaction."

Berti said his job, the same as for everyone in the military, was to prepare for an external attack. Now, with Hoxha gone, everyone was worried that their enemies might invade Albania. "We were told the enemy had not attacked us before because they realized our strength," he added, "and we believed the Party's word because we believed they would never lie to us."

Albania's people had certainly prepared themselves to defend the country. They had built nearly a million pillboxes or bunkers, which scarred the face of the country like concrete acne, from where they would try to repel the invaders with their machine guns. Under every home, school, office, and collective farm were tunnels where people could hide. "There was a national saying," recalled Berti: "We are three million Albanians; we are three million soldiers ready to die to protect our achievements."

From the age of fifteen every student, boy and girl, had to spend four weeks every year, for four years, going to the hills for military training. After leaving high school, all boys had to do two years' military service, or three years if they were sent to join the Marines on Sazan Island. All citizens also had four weeks' military training every year until they were fifty-five years old.

Even then they were expected to help with civil defence. Only children under fourteen, mothers with babies, and retired people could go into the tunnels in the event of an attack, and they all had a specific place and plan. Those over fifty-five years old were expected to be first aiders, nurses, or food providers to those in the tunnels.

Many tunnels were small and self-contained, like Second World War air raid shelters in Britain, while some were interconnected, and others were like small towns underground with communication centres and hospitals for the country's government and military leaders. Every so often bugles were sounded all over the country to test the people's readiness, and they would have to drop everything and take up their military positions. The government would also report to the nation any border incidents, which happened sometimes in the south with Greece, as a warning of the military dangers.

With the country on the highest alert, Berti's first job was to check all his radios were working, particularly those connected to the four commanders who were looking after the Lushnjë zone. He was very satisfied to find every radio and link was working perfectly. Next, he opened up communications on all the radios, which for most the time were closed down, and checked all the orders and communication codes were ready. Finally, he ensured all the weapons at the base were in working order.

The following day, Friday 12 April, Alma and all the students throughout the country reported back to school. She said the normal uniform was a black dress and a white tie, but they had all taken off their ties as a mark of respect. "First, our teacher tried to read the newspapers to us," said Alma, "but she was crying so much that she asked one of my friends to finish reading the articles. I couldn't believe she made my friend read those words."

A week of national mourning was declared. Every school opened a book for pupils to submit their poems and songs about Enver Hoxha, with the teachers deciding which were the best ones. "Thousands and thousands of people wrote poems," said Alma, who wrote quite a few herself, and one of hers was selected for her school's book. "They all promised," she said, "that we would continue to walk in his steps and we would never betray his ideal. Others wrote, 'Why did he die? Albania needed him so. I wish I could have died instead of him'."

That same day Hoxha's body was laid in state in Tirana. Thousands of people travelled from all over Albania, despite the lack of transport. They came by whatever trains and buses they could, to form an orderly queue and walk through the military guard of honour to pay their respects.

Although Berti wasn't called upon for military duty in Tirana, he stayed at his base as the country remained on high alert for the next five days. Alma, too, didn't go to Tirana, but continued with her studies.

The country continued to honour its leader, renaming his birthday, 16 October, Enver Hoxha Day, which then became an Enver Hoxha week. The leader's daughter, Primavera, designed the Enver Hoxha memorial, which was opened in 1988 in the centre of Tirana on the eightieth anniversary of his birth. The dramatic structure, which was nicknamed the Pyramid because of its similarity to the Egyptian buildings, contained everything connected with the leader's life. In the centre was a huge marble statue of the leader himself.

Berti will never forget Thursday 11 April 1985, and not just because of Hoxha's death – it was his twenty-eighth birthday. "It was the strangest birthday of my life," recalled Berti. "Outside my family no one knew it was my birthday and no one, including myself, dared celebrate it."

A couple of thousand miles away Stephen Bell, a grammar school-educated Lancashire lad, an avid Manchester City fan, and a vicar's son was spending Easter on a house party with a missionary group, the European Christian Mission (ECM), at their headquarters, Heightside, in Rawtenstall, Lancashire. He had felt called to go to Albania as a missionary, but that had been impossible with the border closed to outsiders. ECM had suggested he went to Prishtina University in Kosovo and meet Albanians there. Next morning, on Thursday 11 April, at 7:30 a.m., he again prayed and asked for a clear sign from God that he was meant to go to Albania. Then, as he normally did every day, he switched on for the 8 a.m. news on Radio 4. The first item was the announcement of the death of Enver Hoxha. "That was enough for me," said Stephen. "I knew then that I was going to Albania."

But what was the European Christian Mission? Why was it interested in Albania? That story began more than 100 years ago in a remote part of the Russian empire, with the Raud family from Estonia.

Chapter 6

FROM RUSSIA WITH LOVE

Christmas 1903 was a severe winter in Estonia, which was then a backwater of the Russian Empire ruled by Tsar Nicholas II. However, that didn't stop Pertel Raud, a landowner who had been converted to Christianity when he was twenty-six by reading the Bible, taking two of his sons on a ten-day preaching tour in his country.

A huge economic gap existed between the lifestyle of the rich aristocracy and the crushing poverty experienced by the common people. The powerful Orthodox Church persecuted "dissenters". At the end of the nineteenth century, revival within the Lutheran Church in Scandinavia had touched the Baltic states. Even so, for Protestants to preach the gospel in places such as Estonia was to invite trouble, with meetings broken up and preachers arrested, while believers faced intimidation and discrimination.

The Raud family was not put off by these dangers, and on New Year's Eve 1903 they came to a town where a meeting had been arranged in a large private house. The plan was for Pertel to speak first, followed by his son Wil and then by 25-year-old Ganz, the youngest of the five sons.

The meeting, which had started at 8 p.m., had gone well, and it was quite late when Ganz got up to preach on the Judgment of the Great White Throne. Just as he started, the house was raided by the secret police, who had come to arrest the preachers. Before they took the trio away, amazingly, the police allowed Ganz to finish his sermon. Moreover, the police captain was so challenged by Ganz's preaching that he was converted, and the other officers left without making any arrests.

The police captain wasn't the only one converted that night: thirty-nine others were, and a number of the believers there were so thankful that they agreed to spend the rest of the night in prayer. It was in the early hours of 1904 that Ganz felt through prayer called to serve God in Europe. He looked back on that evening and morning as the beginning of the work of the mission he was later to start, the European Christian Mission.

Born in 1878, Ganz became a Christian when he was ten years old, and he soon learnt to stand up for his faith despite the jeers and taunts of other boys at boarding school. His mother used to give him a new Bible every year and he had always read it from cover to cover by the time the next new one arrived. "When I was eighteen," he recalled in *Sharing Christ's Love in Europe*,[1] "I stood at a crossroads. Some friends urged me to pursue academic training, but my father and others were praying that my life might be given to the Lord's work, not the things of this world."

Over the next four years, he spent more time preaching, giving out tracts and visiting hospitals. He felt a burden for Europe, and especially for Great Britain and North America. One day Ganz received an unexpected invitation to hear a German Bible teacher speak in a baron's castle in Tallinn, the capital of Estonia. The teacher encouraged Ganz to leave Estonia and offered him financial support to get more Bible training. Just as

Ganz was planning to leave Estonia, he became so ill that he heard the doctors and his family discussing his funeral.

He recovered, but that wasn't the end of the obstacles put in his way. Some older Christians thought he was too young to go abroad and gave him money for his return fare home. However, he was determined to go, and left early in 1904, an opportune time as a general strike was soon to sweep throughout Russia and revolution was in the air.

To ensure he wasn't tempted to come back home, he quickly spent the money given for his return ticket. For the next ten years he travelled extensively in Europe, setting up interdenominational prayer groups wherever he went. In June 1904 he arrived in Britain to see at first hand the effects of the Welsh Revival.

Although he never attended Bible school, Ganz was tempted to take a course in philosophy at a German university. At the same time he suffered from food poisoning and became critically ill. However, as he recovered and became physically strong he decided he must concentrate on God's call to Europe and America. In the summer of 1914, three weeks before the outbreak of war, Ganz went to the Russian Consul in Berlin to renew his visa. Aware that war was imminent, the consul advised him to return to Estonia at once. There his brother Wil and his father continued to encourage their Estonian congregations to build mission halls, known as "Prayer Houses", and even the Sunday school children were involved in making bricks. Despite this, the family felt that Ganz should go to America to tell the needs of Europe to Christians there. After he was granted a passport, he set out on the hazardous wartime journey to America, via Sweden, Norway, and England.

Both father and son knew they would probably never see each other again on earth, so it was a poignant farewell at the railway station. Ganz recalled: "On the train my father lifted up his hands and like a patriarch gave me his blessing. His last words were: 'God will lead you and keep you, my son, wherever He sends you. Be of good cheer. Let your life be always well pleasing to Him. Let Jesus be the first and last in everything. Do not seek riches, or honour, or glory from men; seek only God's glory and the salvation of souls.'"

With that, Ganz left Estonia in February 1915, and never saw his father again. Pertel Raud died in 1918.

Ganz sailed for America on one of the last journeys of the *Lusitania*, reaching New York, where he knew nobody. However, at a Bible study in the city he met a young couple, Mr and Mrs Thomas McDonald, and it led to a lifetime of service together. Together they founded a mission which they registered as the Russian and Slavonic Bible Union since Ganz's work then was mainly among Slavic people. It had three aims: ministry in Europe, training courses to prepare candidates for working in Europe, and a printing press to produce literature. In 1921 the name of the Bible Union was changed to the European Christian Mission, and in 1922 the mission headquarters moved to Brooklyn, New York. It was in New York again, this time in 1924, that Ganz married one of the mission staff, Miss Elsa Overton, a gifted writer and Bible teacher. In 1927 Thomas McDonald accompanied Ganz on a visit to England, when they registered the mission in London and rented offices, first in London and later at a house in Beulah Hill.

Following the end of the First World War the map of Europe had changed dramatically, with old dynasties swept away and nine new countries appearing almost overnight. There were new opportunities in Central Europe, and the work of

ECM began to expand as missionaries from North America and Britain joined national workers. At first ECM concentrated on providing food and clothing and then Bibles to countries such as Russia. By 1923 there were fifty-five ECM missionaries working in ten European countries. Within four years this had grown to eighty-one missionaries, 243 national helpers, 132 meeting halls, 300 regular gatherings, Bible study courses in four languages and thousands being converted.

In his annual mission report in 1937 Ganz said the mission's work was growing in Spain, France, Austria, Czechoslovakia, Poland, Estonia (where his brother Wil had been the mission director until he died in 1935), Germany, and the Soviet Union. Like his father, Ganz had a special burden for the Jews, and in the years leading up to the Second World War new workers were appointed to work among Jews in Austria, Hungary, and Lithuania. Ganz was asked to speak at a Jewish synagogue in Eastern Europe as long as he didn't mention the name of Jesus. So he preached on the Lamb of God.

When its London headquarters was bombed during the war and the training centre in Penarth, South Wales, was too small to accommodate the growing number of students preparing to go to Europe, the mission contacted all their supporters, saying it was looking for new premises. One supporter mentioned Heightside, near Rawtenstall, Lancashire, formerly the home of a Lancashire businessman and now a Christian conference centre and guesthouse.

Six years later, 1953 saw the close of one chapter and the opening of another. Despite recent ill health, Ganz Raud felt strong enough to begin a trip to Europe in the late summer. After visiting five countries, he arrived exhausted in Paris. On

Saturday 3 October, having suffered a heart attack, he was found unconscious, with his head resting on his own Bible, open at Psalm 143. He died later in hospital.

The same year Heightside became the rented headquarters of ECM in Britain, and eight years later they took it over when Colonel Bolton, the original owner, gave it to the mission. With its move to Rawtenstall ECM expanded its work, introducing an annual Easter conference at Heightside.

In 1961, ECM decided the best way to preach the gospel to those countries behind the Iron Curtain was by radio. When Albania declared itself the world's first atheistic state in 1967, there were those who could not sit idly and do nothing. Programmes were sent from the Rawtenstall studio to Trans World Radio in Monte Carlo, which was sponsored to beam Christian programmes into "godless" Albania, with the first one transmitted on 5 July 1968. One of their many secret listeners would be Captain Berti Dosti, and two of the people who would play a major part in his spiritual journey were Stephen Bell and his friend Gani Smolica.

Chapter 7

WE BOTH CHANGED EACH OTHER'S LIVES

Few students would put Prishtina University, in Kosovo, in their list of the top ten places in the world where they would like to study. Surrounded by 300-metre hills, Prishtina, the state capital, lies in a valley, with towering, ugly 1960s concrete buildings, characterless blocks of flats and chaotic traffic problems. It can be a forbidding place, with tensions between the Serbs and the majority Albanians just below the surface. When Albania had been declared an independent but smaller sovereign state under international guarantee in July 1913, more than half of the Albanians were left outside the new borders in places such as Kosovo, which remained part of Yugoslavia. Sometimes the tension came out into the open, as in June 1989, when riots and shooting broke out and the authorities responded by banning all public meetings of more than three people.

One of Prishtina's most important places is the university, which has 60,000 students out of a population of 200,000. An unusual student who arrived there on 14 August 1986 was Stephen Bell, who hardly spoke a word of Albanian and so couldn't understand much of the lectures. It didn't help that sometimes the lecturers moved rooms at the last minute, and he couldn't translate the scruffy notes put on the doors telling students of the new location.

Dates and times of exams were another problem. The university authorities didn't like to reveal them until the last possible minute, which didn't help Stephen in his revision or his holiday plans to go home to England. In addition, 27-year-old Stephen, who had enrolled in the linguistics and philosophy faculty for five years, was different to the other students – many of whom were young Greeks dodging their military call-up. Not only was he older than most of them, but also he did his best to fail the exams, so that he could stay in Prishtina as long as possible to improve his language skills. When Stephen told the other students he was hoping to go and work in Albania, they all laughed and said, "There is no hope of Albania opening up to foreigners."

The real reason why he was there was that he was a missionary working with ECM to follow up listeners to Albanian radio broadcasts, as well as learning Albanian. He wouldn't be allowed into the country if he put missionary on his visa application, so he put student – and to do that he needed to stay at the university. However, no matter how hard he tried to fail the exams, the authorities, who were mystified by Stephen and thought he must be a spy, still gave him exam passes. The police interrogated his friends, asking them, "Who is Stephen? What is he doing here?"

Between July and August 1990, Stephen was aware that eleven of his friends had been called in for questioning, though he wonders how many more were quizzed and didn't tell him. Stephen also knew his phone was bugged and his mail was opened. Bizarrely, on his course Stephen had to take a second language – they tried to make him learn German – and when he plumped for Serbo-Croat, as it was at least of some practical use, he was told he couldn't do that because it wasn't a foreign language. So he had to study English and he even had to take an exam in it in his second year. Not surprisingly, he did so well that he ended up giving the lectures. Finally, Stephen, who is still proud of his pass in Marxism, decided the only way to ensure he failed was not to turn up for some of the exams – and he managed to stay there for five years and complete and pass the course.

However, the 27-year-old Lancashire student had found it quite difficult and lonely at first settling down to life in Prishtina, particularly as he had never lived away from home for so long. "Occasionally," he admitted, "I did feel fed up, bored, and isolated." For the first year he lived with an Albanian professor of French and his family, and then for the next four years he stayed with another Albanian family and their four children. It wasn't easy living in Prishtina, where temperatures varied from 40°C to minus 20°C, and the fact that the city was in a valley meant he had to climb up 124 steps every night to get home. Although the family were hospitable, his only space was his three metres by four metres room, and there were few places to escape to, as the police ordered all the shops, restaurants, and cafés to close by 10 p.m.

He did go to the local cinema occasionally, but his favourite bolthole was the Grand Hotel in the city centre. They had posh toilets, and he could order a coffee and read the British newspapers, sent out by his parents from England, before falling asleep for a couple of hours in the comfortable chairs. As the post took two weeks to arrive, the papers were out of date, but they still enabled Stephen to keep up to date with his beloved Manchester City.

However, Stephen was determined to make the best of the opportunity, and that meant learning the language as soon as possible. Every day he would go to university lectures from 7 a.m. until noon. On his way home, he invented a game whereby he couldn't go up the next of the 124 steps until he had said an Albanian word. His aim was to learn twenty new words a day, every day. To improve his language skills, he spent at least an hour a day evangelizing in Albanian to anyone who would listen.

Every Saturday he and Shau Ping, a Chinese student who had also come to Prishtina to learn Albanian, would go to a different town to practise their new language. It was a great encouragement for Stephen that Shau Ping became a Christian after the first two months. As well as making friends with Shau Ping, Stephen went to the local Pentecostal church, which had been built only a year before. Here he met an American missionary couple, the Serbian pastor and his wife, and an Albanian Bible college student, together with just one Albanian believer. Shau Ping also made quite a difference, even writing Christian songs in Albanian, English, and Chinese!

Stephen found many Albanians to talk to in the town, and slowly he became more confident with the language. With annual trips home and friends and family coming out to see him, he soon adapted to life in Prishtina.

His journey to Prishtina had really begun in Leigh, Lancashire. Born in Ardwick, Manchester, on 19 May 1959, he went to school in Bolton. As a teenager, Stephen became very keen on football and less keen on having to go to church at Mosley Common as the vicar's son. He was surprised when his brother, David, came home from university one day and said he had become a Christian. "But you've always been one," Stephen told him. The younger brother was even more puzzled when David started going to a Christian youth group a few miles away in Leigh on Sunday nights and then reported that he had even been invited to play in their football team! "I wanted to play in the team, but I was too proud to go to the youth group and ask," said Stephen.

Then, when the Easter holidays came round and David returned from university, Stephen nonchalantly asked him if he was going to "that youth group again". When David said yes, Stephen asked if he could go with him. Stephen was introduced to the captain of the football team, Philip Butterworth, who was to become a good friend and who played a part in the Albania story. Stephen joined the team and regularly attended the meetings. As summer approached, he was invited to go with the group to a Christian camp near Lulworth Cove in Dorset with around 150 young people, and there he became a Christian.

At the youth group, he heared a speaker from Underground Evangelism, a Christian organization helping the persecuted church in Eastern Europe. He was so angry hearing about pastors killed and Bibles banned that when he left school and joined the NatWest Bank in 1978, he immediately pledged £10 a month to help the persecuted Christians.

When Stephen was offered the bank job, he also made a pact with God. He had noticed that many people had been on fire for God in their youth, but as they got a job and settled down, they seemingly lost their enthusiasm for Christianity. As a guarantee against mediocrity, he said that he would regularly seek God's will and be ready to give up his job if that was God's desire, and after five years he would specifically seek God's will for the future. As the five years ended, it became clear to Stephen that he really was to go to Eastern Europe.

His father Jack was delighted his younger son wanted to be a missionary. He had been all set to go to China in 1949, but was prevented as the Communist authorities had just seized power and were forcing the foreign Christians to leave the country. But even Jack was slightly concerned about Stephen's next plan – to become a Bible smuggler with Open Doors. "I had spent years praying and preaching for people to be called to missionary service and go, but now it hit home when it was my son going," he said.

Stephen took two weeks' leave from the bank in June 1983 to go on one trip behind the Iron Curtain, smuggling Bibles in black bin bags to Romania. When his team arrived in Bucharest, many of the police were diverted to an incident in another part of the city, allowing the visitors to meet their contact in relative safety. "We met these Romanian Christians in the dark and handed over the Bibles. I remember getting a kiss on both cheeks from a half-shaven Romanian and being given a vase which my mum Elsie still has," recalled Stephen. "But there was no other personal contact."

Jack was still trying to steer Stephen towards ECM, having been involved with the organization all his life, and arranged for his son to go to the 1983 ECM Easter conference and meet the leaders. The advice given was that Stephen should join a short-term summer team working in Eastern Europe and then prepare for future involvement by going to theological college. Stephen said there was no way he was going to study liberal theology. "You go in as Billy Graham, and you leave as the Bishop of Durham," was his view. This was at a time when the then Bishop of Durham had questioned the miracle of the resurrection.

However, Stephen did quit the bank after five years and did listen to older Christians' advice, successfully applying to join All Nations College in Ware, Hertfordshire, in September 1983. "The two years there were the best years of my life," he said. Just before he finished at college, Stephen went to the 1985 ECM Easter conference at Heightside, Rawtenstall. In a room of around 300 people, one of the leaders prophesied: "Somebody in this room has got the call to go to my Albania." The speaker was Sali Rahmani, the broadcaster from Trans World Radio whom Captain Berti Dosti had heard while on duty in the Albanian army. "I was very careful to not get carried along with the emotional sway, and so sought a clear sign," recalled Stephen. That sign came a few days later when he switched on the 8 a.m. news and heard that Enver Hoxha had died.

In July 1985, Stephen set off for Vienna and a six-week singing trip to Hungary and Yugoslavia. After the tour, he returned in September to Vienna to discuss the idea of Albania with ECM East European director Tom Lewis. Tom suggested he went to Prishtina, as it was the nearest place to meet Albanians, and he could apply to study at the university there. An experienced ECMer, Doug Groth, was asked to accompany Stephen on a flying two-day visit that September, so he could prepare to apply for the course there a year later.

Before leaving Prishtina, Stephen approached the university principal, Sali Maqedonci, who spoke perfect English. "He was very amused that I was interested in booking a place there a year in advance," recalled Stephen. "He told me to come back in twelve months' time."

"Here in the Balkans," mused Sali, flashing a mischievous smile, "we tend to leave the registration, er... *somewhat later* than you do in England." Indeed, it was even *after* the new term had already started that Stephen could eventually register. No problem: the lectures started even later, in early October!

When his three-month summer with ECM in Eastern Europe was up, Stephen returned to Manchester, where two weeks later he embarked on a two-week visit to Albania with his old friend Phil Butterworth from the Leigh youth group. They travelled by coach from Huddersfield on a trip organized by a Yorkshire Communist miners' group, Yorkshire Tours, which cost just £228. With Enver Hoxha having died only a few months earlier after more than forty years in power, Stephen was surprised that this closed country was welcoming foreign visitors so soon.

Three days and three nights after leaving Huddersfield, and after staying in surprisingly luxurious hotels on the way, the party of twenty-eight arrived in Albania on 4 October 1985. Of his first impressions of Albania, Stephen said, "I could not help but be shocked at the primitive standards of farming. As the official bus trundled along the dusty roads I saw crops failing, withering in the sun. I counted up to 500 people, mostly women, working in the fields, toiling in ninety-degree temperatures. I did spot some tractors and harvesters, but they were very few. As we drove into the towns, the drabness was striking. Buildings were mostly dilapidated and pale in colour. Shops, having neither adverts nor window displays, were difficult to locate, and when I entered some, the items on sale were very basic. Food was very scarce, and meat was impossible to find outside our hotel dining rooms.

"I saw one shop selling cookers that were obsolete in Britain years ago, yet in every town there was a bookshop with stacks of books, mostly the works of Enver Hoxha, on display. I was reliably informed that due to a paper shortage and their 'popularity' 95 per cent of them would be recycled unsold, for other uses." Stephen later found out, when he started living in Albania in 1991, that they were used as toilet paper!

He added, "The towns were characterized by their

abundance of idle people and the absence of traffic." While on a walkabout in Durres, the main port and second largest city in Albania, he said, "I could see people, notably men, milling in public places, squares etc. This grew to a crescendo from 6 p.m. onwards, when the Albanians went on walkabout, a cultural habit which leaves certain streets chock-a-block with wandering humanity. At first I was stared at, clearly a foreigner, almost as if I were an alien from Mars, but as the night rapidly drew in I grew more inconspicuous and merged into the crowd.

"I've only experienced one other walkabout – in Kosovo, just across the border. The contrast was that while in Kosovo the streets seemed alive with a bubbling, vibrant populace, the scene in Albania was subdued, the smiles replaced by impassive, sullen faces – the noise replaced by relative silence. The poverty of the place was obvious. Most people wore simple, well-worn clothes of an outdated style, and some people looked distinctly underfed. For toys, it seemed the young children had to be satisfied with bits of wood and metal that they had found. I never once saw a child clutching a toy car, doll, or other manufactured article. Vehicles were limited to lorries struggling along the dirt tracks, private cars were banned, and the lucky people who owned bicycles had the freedom of the roads."

Stephen saw some old Eastern European cars in Tirana, but the Albturist guide admitted that only Party members used them. He took trips to various places, including a cotton factory, a concert, and a school, and all the time they were passing military pillboxes. There were signs everywhere declaring the praises of the dead leader Enver Hoxha, yet Stephen's impression was, "There doesn't seem all that much to shout about." Of the factory they visited, he said, "It was noisy and smelly, and the looms and other machinery were imported in the 1960s from the Chinese and looked dilapidated. A mechanic friend told me there were drastically few safety devices. We were also told by the supervisor that the workforce worked round the clock to maximize output, but I heard a conflicting report that many factories were now on a two-day week, because of the lack of electricity, with the workers laid off and unpaid."

Of the school visit, he said, "The first one we visited was a kindergarten for ages three to six. I was frightened for the children when they all trooped out in single file, stamping their feet, saluting with clenched fist to the pulse of their shouts of 'Enver Hoxha! Enver Hoxha!' On the way back we had the privilege of passing a wedding procession on the road. The bridegroom and his new bride were slowly walking along the country road, accompanied by an accordionist, violinist, and singers. The crowd of eighty or so guests were dancing around them. It was a unique opportunity to see such a sight, and my heart warmed to see a little happiness in this bleak country."

Finally, Stephen said, "Radios seemed plentiful, and bearing in mind ECM's daily radio broadcasts via Trans World Radio in Monte Carlo, I was encouraged by what I saw. Apparently most Albanians preferred foreign radio broadcasts to the incessant propaganda on Albanian TV and radio."

What the left-wing Yorkshire miners thought of Stephen and Phil, who were so different in education, background, and outlook, they never found out. However, they did discover one day what one of the others thought. An English journalist who had gone incognito to write a travel report for a national British newspaper suddenly asked them, "Are you real? You're Christians, aren't you?" "What do you mean?" replied Stephen. "I've been watching you two," said the journalist. "You don't swear, you don't smoke, you don't get drunk, you don't chase the girls, you're too nice."

They thought it was too dangerous then to admit publicly that they were Christians. However, they continued to talk to their two tour guides, Andre and Anton, who wanted to practise their English and, as single men, were desperate to leave Albania. Before leaving Durres the tour party also challenged the locals to a beach game of football, with Albania beating England 2-0. They visited Berat, Tirana, and Krujé before the long coach ride back home to Huddersfield. Stephen said, "It's an amazing country – one I would not like to live in, yet if God made it possible I would go there." He was also relieved to read the journalist's report about the Albanian trip in a Sunday paper and to find there was no mention of himself nor his friend Phil Butterworth.

That trip convinced Stephen to return to Prishtina a year later to enrol at the university. But in the meantime, as he had to wait, he went to work at St Andrew's in Plaistow, East London, for seven months to prepare himself for Kosovo and to get further training in church-based evangelism before flying out for a two-week language course at Prishtina on 14 August. He was the only British person on the language course; the other sixty were mostly Communists. Stephen couldn't get over the Kosovans' generosity, as they provided free meals, free accommodation in a student dormitory, and free education with five hours of Albanian language teaching every day. In the afternoon, they were taken to the Kosovan sites – for free.

On 29 August, the day after the course finished, Stephen began life on his own with his Albanian phrasebook, a little knowledge of Albanian, and a place in the queue to enrol at Prishtina University. But he couldn't understand what the enrolling officer was saying to him. As he looked round wondering what to do next, a young Kosovan, Gani Smolica, who was next in the queue and who would later become a key person in Berti's story, said to him in a perfect Oxford English accent, "Excuse me, can I help you?"

Gani really shouldn't have been in that queue to enrol at Prishtina University that day. He was, in fact, a professor who by day taught young medical students and during the evening translated for TV and radio companies to earn some extra money. He was there because his wife Adile needed to take a university exam, and she thought it was easier for her husband to sort out the paperwork.

Gani was born on 25 September 1958 in the beautiful town on Peja, which lies at the foot of the mountains. It is the gateway to Montenegro and famous for being the home of the Serbian Orthodox Church. His father, who was a shoemaker in a factory, and his mother were nominally Communist. When Gani was twelve, the family moved to Prishtina because of his father's work. He proved to be an excellent linguist and learned to speak English from the age of eleven. Eventually he could speak French and a little Russian, as well as Serbian and Albanian.

He went to Prishtina University, where he met two people who were to have a big influence on his life, although there was a gap of ten years between the two events. First, in 1976, he was introduced to a young student, Adile, when they went to the same group of lectures to study English language and literature. Adile, who was born on 2 January 1959, came from Peja, where her father was the director of a small company. Her mother died when she was only eight years old. The two students became friends, and five years later, in 1981, Gani and Adile were married. By the time they met Stephen, they already had two daughters, Besiana and Doruntina. They were later to have two sons, Lorik and Shpetim.

The second event was in 1986. After Gani had helped Stephen enrol at university they used to meet for Coca Cola and kebabs, and would help each other to improve their English and Albanian. "For five or six months this Englishman kept talking to me about Jesus, but I didn't want to listen," said Gani. "He even gave me a Bible to help me with my English." It was three years later, when Gani had a pizza with Stephen and a Brazilian woman missionary called Nazhua, that he decided enough of his questions had been answered for him to become a Christian. In December 1989, Stephen and the church pastor baptized him.

"I did notice a difference," said Adile. "Gani became a better husband and he started looking after the children more and helping around the house." But Adile wasn't interested in Christianity, as she was pregnant with Lorik. Money was tight, and she wondered whether they could afford a third child. "Then I read a book that said as soon as a child is conceived it is a human being, and that made me think," she said. Then, after talking with Stephen and Nazhua over a long time, Adile too became a believer in January 1989.

That chance meeting between Stephen and Gani at Prishtina University was the start of a lifelong friendship, and, as Stephen said, "We both changed each other's lives."

Chapter 8

A HIGH POINT – AND A LOW POINT

Although Enver Hoxha had died in 1985, nothing really changed in Albania for the next four years. His chosen successor, Ramiz Alia, who was the leader of the Party of Labour, the Communist Party, continued with the one-party state and used the army to keep order.

Although Berti had become an officer when he was older than many of his colleagues, his military record and expertise were not in question. He proved this when he was the star soldier during a big military exercise in Kavaja in 1986. Every kind of weapon was on show, and Berti's communications were rated as first-class, particularly as he had introduced new ideas and ways of using radio communications.

The top brass in the Albanian army noticed Berti's skills, and the exercise was such a success that he was presented with the Urdhëri i Shërbimit Ushtarak të Klasit III, the third-highest military medal in the country, on 8 July 1986. The citation said the medal was for "distinguished work in organization and leadership in the military base where he served and for attaining very high achievements of practice with his fellow soldiers". The medal was signed by the top general and the first secretary of the Albanian army, and was presented at the Kavaja army headquarters in the presence of officers only.

It was a tremendous achievement for someone who had been an officer for only three years and who was not yet thirty years old. His father must have been proud of Berti, who by now had eclipsed his father's military record and that of his brother Iliri. However, unlike the case with the British army, Albanian soldiers are not presented with such honours with pomp and ceremony in front of family members. In those days, the army was a very secret and closed place, even to Albanians. Berti's father, who had now retired from the military, was not allowed inside the base. If any Albanian who was not a full-time soldier stumbled across a military location, he or she could be arrested and accused of spying.

Nevertheless, although Berti had an impeccable military record, he was about to blot his party biography again.

He decided that if he was to get promotion, he needed to become a member of the Party, which with his background should have been a formality. Only the best could become Party members, and if they asked to be admitted to membership, officials would investigate very carefully every aspect of the person and his or her family. They would go back to the third and fourth generations and see how devoted the applicant and their family were to the Party. If a person had long hair or the fashionable drainpipes trousers, that person had been tempted by foreign influences. If they were well educated, smartly dressed and knew another language, they were labelled foreign intellectuals, which would count against them. If they showed an interest in world news or TV or foreign films, that could also mean minus points against their name.

Everyone watched everyone else in Albania. There was a web of spies, and people would sell information, real or invented, to the authorities. Berti knew he was being watched, but he waited for the Party to tell him whether he had been successful. He knew members were called to a prestigious ceremony in the Party's meeting room, attended by the secretary of the Party and other VIPs, at which all loyal Party members were seated on a podium at the front of the hall.

The candidate was kept outside while his or her proposer addressed the Party members and put the case for the person to be admitted to the Party. The irony was that the officials were too afraid to reject anyone, in case it reflected badly on them and their career. Then the person was called into the room, where he or she said what an honour it was and promised that they would work day and night for the Party. They swore they would be ready to give their life for the sake of the Party and that they would be "first in sacrificing and last in pretending". They would also be prepared to work anywhere in the country. If the officials suspected he or she had any intellectual leanings, they would be sent out into the country and given a lowly-paid job there. However, Berti thought he would be protected from all that with his military background.

By now, Berti had his own office at the base, the only one who did, and it contained the treasured possession of a black and white TV. In Albania permission was needed to buy a TV, as their number was limited, and only people of good standing could have one. It was the same with going to university, getting a job or a house: people needed a good biography and Party approval. Those who did not have a "clean biography" ended up squashed into a one-roomed house with no luxuries.

One evening it had been a long, 24-hour shift and as usual, nothing had happened. The airwaves were quiet; the base was deserted as there was only Berti and a guard duty soldier working. He was feeling tired, it was 1 a.m., and he thought he would switch on the TV. He started to watch *Boot Hill*, a cowboy film – but he could only understand a little as it was in Italian.

Suddenly, two officials quietly came into the office without knocking – the Commissar and the base Commandant. Berti was accused of two mistakes: first, watching a foreign TV station, and second, not doing his duty. Although he wasn't asleep, he hadn't been walking around the base to check on the soldier on guard duty. If he had, he would have found, just as the Commissar and Commandant had, that there was no one guarding the base. What Berti didn't realize was that the soldier was in the shadows outside his office, quietly watching the same film with him through a window.

The next day Berti was told he was going to be fined for his early morning misdemeanours. Although he had not committed a huge mistake, he was so bitter and angry that he didn't go in to work for three days. Then when he returned to the Suzoltaj base one of his friends, an officer, said, "What have you done wrong? I have heard your name mentioned in discussions a lot. You were close to being accepted to become a Party member, but now you are going to be rejected."

Although it was a bad offence to be criticized at the base, it was far more serious when it went to the Party. Berti was so furious he went to see the Commissar and challenged him: "Why did you tell the Party, and why haven't you told me they have rejected me from becoming a member?" The Commissar replied, "It was my duty to tell the truth to the Party." "But it wasn't such a serious offence that it had to go to the Party," retorted Berti.

"It is my duty to inform the Party of everything," he replied. With that the conversation ended. The duty soldier received only a criticism, while Berti never did hear officially that the Party had rejected him.

A while later Berti remembered the TV incident as he thought about what he had heard on the radio while he was twiddling the dials. "If you want to find out more about God, we will meet again tomorrow," said the presenter one night in late 1989. Berti was intrigued – but dare he take the chance? It was bad enough to be caught watching a cowboy film in Italian, but to be found listening to a Christian radio programme would be a second, and far more serious, offence. God was never mentioned while he was at school, so why should a fifteen-minute programme from the enemy in the West intrigue him? To this day, he doesn't know why, although "something deep down was telling me to listen". He added, "Religion was a total mystery, but I wanted to find out more, particularly about creation."

Berti knew the risks of being caught and losing his job, and the effect this would have on his family, particularly as by now Berti and Tatjana had a second child, a son, Dorian, born on 23 April 1988. So he decided to talk to Tatjana about the idea. "I was worried," she admitted, "but I have always supported Berti and knew he would be very careful." Berti thought it was a risk worth taking, and remembering what had happened in the TV incident, he used his military brain to minimize as many of the dangers as possible. He knew the programme came on at 8:45 p.m., when he would again be alone in the base, with just a soldier on guard duty.

First, he checked the soldier was on duty at the entrance to the base and told him to phone through immediately if there were any visitors whatsoever. Then he walked into his office, which was only about three metres by three metres and was full of radios, and carefully shut the door. At least he would hear anyone coming into his office this time. He went to his desk, put on his headphones, and settled back to tune in to Trans World Radio. With the TV, there was no remote control, so he could not change channels easily if someone walked in. However, with the radio he could move the dial easily. Even better, if someone did see him with his headphones on, as they were most of the day when he was on duty, they would presume he was doing his job of protecting Albania's defences from a surprise attack.

The programme asked "Who is God?" – a question Berti had never considered before. The presenter finished by saying, "If you want to find out more, write to me, Luan Mateu, at PO Box 349, Monte Carlo, Monaco." However, it was a while before Berti would pluck up the courage to write to the radio station. What he didn't know then and would find out much later was that the address was a postbox for Trans World Radio, and Luan Mateu was a *nom de plume*. He was, in fact, Sali Rahmani, born in Kosovo, who was now recording the programmes in England, where he worked for the European Christian Mission, the organization that had already influenced Stephen Bell.

How did Trans World Radio end up broadcasting into atheistic and Communist Albania from capitalist Monaco? That story begins when an American arrived in Spain in 1948.

Chapter 9

MONTE CARLO – AND NEARLY BUST

Spain was the last place on earth American Paul E. Freed wanted to be on that muggy day in 1948. The thirty-year-old had been persuaded to go to the International Youth for Christ Conference in Beatenberg, Switzerland, where two zealous Spaniards invited him back to Barcelona for a short visit to discuss how they could reach 30 million people with the gospel in the second most mountainous country in Europe. The more Paul thought about it, the more he realized radio was the only answer. "But I did not have a dime of support," he said.[1]

Paul, whose parents were missionaries in southern Syria, was educated in Jerusalem and Beirut before he returned to America to go to Wheaton College, Illinois, and Nyack Missionary Training Institute, New York, where his father had enrolled almost twenty years earlier. In 1948 he became Youth for Christ director in Greensboro, North Carolina, and it was there that the movement's founder, Torrey Johnson, persuaded him to go to the conference in Switzerland, which ended with the detour to Spain.

When he returned from Spain he resigned from Youth for Christ, became an evangelist and set up a business designing and building trailers and homes, which he thought could become a good financial basis to realize his radio dream. It wasn't until 1951 that Paul took his wife Betty Jane to Spain for the first time, where a Spanish interpreter told them, "You ought to go over to Tangier: that's the best place for broadcasting." The next day they went to Morocco to visit an eighty-year-old English missionary, Mr Elson, who owned some land and a small cottage. When Paul suggested to him the possibility of giving the old mission property for gospel radio, he replied, "Young man, if you can give your life for mission, the least I can do is give my property." He discussed it with his relatives and they came up with a compromise price of 15,000 dollars, way below its real value. They now knew they could start a radio station and its address would be Tangier, but how could they get the support of American Christians?

Paul and Betty Jane returned to the USA and produced a film, *Banderilla*, about the project. For two and a half months the couple, now with two young children, went on an 11,000-mile deputation trip. They got plenty of support but little money for the radio station. Nevertheless, on 11 February 1952 they founded Trans World Radio, under the name International Evangelism – the same day that their third child, Donna Jean, was born. But how were they going to run the station?

Critics were quick to point out it didn't exist yet, there was no board of directors and no long-term plan, it wasn't linked to an official missionary group, and anyway, why start yet another radio station? Despite the opposition, the Freeds, with their three children under five years old, decided to sell their house and return to Tangier.

Paul's first job was to get the necessary government permit to build the station. As he was walking through the noisy streets of Tangier, an American stopped him and said, "My name is Southworth. I understand you are trying to build a radio station."

Paul knew the man had his own station in the international zone of Tangier, as he continued, "I'd like to suggest that your station be put up under my permit. You may save a year or more in time."

Paul was reluctant at first, but later agreed it was a perfect solution. Mr Southworth would build the transmitters and antennas and then lease the whole package back to them. He had the permit, the land, and the engineering crew, and it would involve a much smaller cash outlay for the Freeds. But what should they do with the beautiful property overlooking the Straits of Gibraltar, which would be ideal for a studio and flats, if they had 15,000 dollars?

Later, when they had returned to the States for a holiday, and while they were riding through the Pennsylvania countryside with a friend, Clarence Staats, they mentioned the property and the price to him. "I don't see why we can't arrange that for you," he said, and later mailed the whole amount to Tangier.

Finally, "The Voice of Tangier", as it came to be known, went on the air in 1954 with a budget of 10,000 dollars for the first year. Ten years later that figure had increased by more than a hundred times. For the first five years, however, it was tough finding money to run the station, as interest in Christian radio was almost non-existent among evangelicals in Europe, and it was just as difficult finding staff to produce the programmes. However, the Freeds persevered and the work continued to grow. In 1956 the old transmitter was replaced, so they were able to broadcast to twenty-four different language groups, beaming specific programmes into almost every country in Europe, North Africa and the Middle East. Then disaster struck. In April 1959 the Moroccan government announced that every radio station in the country was to be nationalized by the end of the year.

At least The Voice of Tangier did have another option. Two years earlier, they had been looking to expand. It was Paul's mother who said to him just six months before she died in November 1957 that he should look at Monte Carlo. Despite what seemed a strange choice, to relocate to probably the wealthiest piece of land in Europe, Paul switched his New York flight the next morning in spring 1957 and headed for Monte Carlo instead. The talks with Radio Monte Carlo executive Erik Bosio on top of the mountain by the antennas that had been put up by Hitler's regime during the war to spread the Nazi propaganda went well, but nothing was decided.

Paul didn't think about Monte Carlo again until the Moroccan Government decision. He decided that he would offer the radio station board an advance of 50,000 dollars towards installing the antenna system and the 100,000-watt transmitter. That is until he met Erik Bosio again, who gave him a reality check. He said the board would want payment of the total amount of 500,000 dollars in advance, that there would be one opportunity on a take-it-or-leave-it basis, and that they would not be interested in investing any of their own funds in the project. The money was to be paid in six instalments, the first when they approved the project and the other five within a year of all the equipment being put up. If any of the instalments were late, the whole project collapsed. "Even the one-sixth figure for the down payment – 83,000 dollars – sounded fantastic," recalled Paul. "I honestly wondered if I had lost my mind."

The board agreed the price and said Paul could lease the radio facility full-time for ten years with an indefinite number of renewals. The next problem was where to find the money, as there was only a month between drawing up the contract in

August 1959 and the next board meeting in September. Earlier in the autumn of 1957, when his mother was in a London hospital with pneumonia, she decided to try to tune in to The Voice of Tangier. She called about twenty people over to listen, including a Norwegian visitor. Later he invited Paul, when he was on his way to Russia, to call in to Norway, where he met the Haanes family, who owned a large shipping company and several other successful businesses. On the day of the board meeting, there was a cheque from the Haanes family – for 83,000 dollars. However, five more payments were still needed. Their bank in New Jersey gave them a deadline for transferring the second payment to Monte Carlo, and on the final day they were still 8,000 dollars short. At 11:30 a.m. Paul said his team, "I'll have to leave for the bank now, or I won't make the deadline." As he drove along, one of the workers walking down the street waved him over, saying he had just picked up a letter at the post office with a cheque for 5,000 dollars in it.

He met the bank president and told him they were still 3,000 dollars short. As they went into the president's office, the phone rang. The president almost dropped the phone. "How in the world can this happen?" he said. "Well, who was it?" stammered Paul. The bank president said a telegram had come from Western Union, wiring funds to the account of Trans World Radio for 3,000 dollars, adding, "I sure wish I knew who sent it." An amazed Paul said quietly, "Well, I know who sent it. God sent it." "Who did you say?" The president leaned over the desk towards him. Still shaking his head, Paul repeated his comment: "God sent it."

"I didn't quite hear you. What was the man's name?" asked the bank official. This time Paul turned to him and repeated slowly and deliberately, "Almighty God sent it." Now the banker shook his head. He said, almost inaudibly, "You know, I believe, you're right."

Money then came in to the radio station for the next three instalments, but there was still one more bank drama to go before the final payment for the Monte Carlo station was complete. The afternoon before the final deadline day they were 1,500 dollars short. The next morning at Barclay's Bank an official told Paul, "No other funds have come in since yesterday. But if you don't mind, I'd like to take a few minutes to refigure it." He returned with a mysterious smile: "You made it."

"What do you mean, we made it?" asked Paul. "You'll never believe it," he said, "but the German mark has jumped in value since we figured the total, which adds exactly 1,500 dollars to your account."

On 16 October 1960, Trans World Radio went on the air, thirteen months after they had signed the contract. The station broadcast in twenty-four different languages, using nationals to record in their own country and send their tapes to Monte Carlo for transmission.

But all this stress had had an effect on Paul's health. Nine months later, in June 1961, he returned to the States for a holiday. While playing tennis he had a serious heart attack at the age of forty-two years and nearly died.

During the first year in Monte Carlo, 18,000 letters arrived at the radio station. Then the station was granted permission to use Radio Monte Carlo's giant 400,000-watt medium wave (standard broadcast) AM transmitter after 10 p.m., so they could reach many homes in the heart of Europe during prime evening hours. By 1967, the number of missionaries and national workers at the radio station was more than 200 adults and nearly 150 children.

In the late 1960s and early 1970s, the broadcasts continued to expand. More and more letters flowed in from every country, apart from Albania, to which they had been broadcasting since 1968. They hadn't had a single letter in reply to Sali Rahmani's programme, and many times Trans World Radio officials must have wondered whether anyone in Albania was listening. No one would know the answer to that question for another twenty-three years.

Chapter 10

ONCE I WAS BLIND BUT NOW I CAN SEE

For the first two years of his life Sali Rahmani couldn't see a thing. Most of his family thought he would be blind for life but his mother, Hanumsha, didn't lose hope that one day he would be able to see. She realized as soon as Sali was born, on 14 April 1946, in Ferizaj in south-eastern Kosovo, near the border with Macedonia, that there was something wrong with his eyes: they didn't seem to respond to movement or noise. She took him to Skopje Hospital and they twice operated on his eyes, but still he couldn't see. Hanumsha knew one of the leading eye experts lived in Greece, so she sold some of their household goods to pay for the trip to Thessalonica, but even that doctor couldn't restore Sali's sight.

However, she still believed that her son would be healed, and so every August from the year Sali was born, she left her family in Ferizaj, or Urosevac as it is known in Serbian, to travel to a Catholic shrine in nearby Letnica for three weeks. She joined thousands of pilgrims of various ethnic and religious backgrounds, including Croatian Catholics, Albanian Catholics, Orthodox Serbs and Albanian and Kosovo Muslims, at the huge white church with two bell towers which stands on a hill and dominates the town. Hanumsha believed that if she prayed before the church's rare black Madonna statue of the Majka Božja Letnica (the Madonna of Letnica) her son would be healed. Some pilgrims who came to worship there said they had seen what appeared to be tears coming from the statue's eyes, while others claimed to have been healed, and childless couples who prayed there later had children.

When Sali was two and a half she took him with her to the shrine for the first time. As he walked round the church on the first day he suddenly pointed with his finger at the famous picture of Jesus the Lamb behind the altar and said, "Look, Mama." Hanumsha couldn't believe it: her son had never pointed at anything in his life before. "Do you see something?" she asked nervously. "Yes," said Sali. She tested him again, asking him to look at other things in the church before being convinced he could now see. "I was told later she nearly passed out with joy; she was convinced it was a miracle," said Sali. They completed the pilgrimage, and a couple of days later returned home for a huge family celebration, where even his father, Hasan, a dedicated Communist, who was very anti-religious, had to accept something had happened to his son.

Sali went with his mother every year on the pilgrimage until he was thirteen, because she was worried that his blindness would return. The doctors couldn't explain what had happened to Sali, except to say he had had serious complications in both eyes as well as cataracts. Afterwards, Hanumsha gave birth to four other children, three sons and a daughter, and they were all born with perfect sight.

Sali wasn't the only pilgrim who had been affected by a visit to the church in Letnica. Years earlier a young girl, Agnes Bojaxhiu, born on 26 August 1910 near Skopje, when it was the administrative capital in Kosovo, had been a regular pilgrim there. She enjoyed the choir's singing and went on several retreats at the church. At the age of seventeen, in the year when her father, an activist in the Albanian nationalist movement, was poisoned in the civil war with Yugoslavia, she dedicated herself to helping the world's poor and hungry. She became a nun, joined the Order of the Loreto sisters, and taught for many years in Calcutta, India, where she was better known as Mother Teresa. In 1946 she founded the Missionaries of Charity, just two years after Enver Hoxha took control of Albania. Ironically, while this Kosovan Albanian Mother Teresa was becoming one of the most famous Christians in the world, another Albanian, Enver Hoxha, was declaring in 1967 that his country was the world's first atheist state.

Mother Teresa outlived Hoxha, and when Albania began to open its borders in 1989 she visited her homeland, and a branch of her Missionaries of Charity was established there a year later. She died in Calcutta in 1997 and was given a state funeral, attended by more than 12,000 mourners.[1]

Sali and his two younger brothers had had a reasonable standard of living in a better than average house, as his father was a police officer. Unlike Albania, where religion was banned, Yugoslavia's President Tito allowed religion to continue in his country, including Kosovo.

Sali's upbringing was strict: there was no swearing, drinking, smoking nor any unkindness allowed. Sali remembers as a youngster punching his friend Tuna Prekpalaj, now a doctor of philosophy in Holland, so hard in the stomach that he fainted. When his mother found out, she was so angry that she threw him across the room into a wall, and to this day he still has a couple of scars to remind him of the incident. But he added, "I never hit anyone again after that."

Sali went to the local school, Tefik Çanga, from the age of six until he was sixteen. It brought back many poignant memories for his father. During the war, he had been a double agent. By day he was a police officer working for the Germans, and by night he worked for the Partisans, the resistance movement. The Germans believed he had infiltrated the Partisans to provide them with information, while he gave the Partisans intelligence about the German invaders. His best friend, Tefik Çanga, also worked as a spy, but he was arrested. The Germans hung him by his feet outside the school in the square and forced the townspeople to watch him die.

However, they never forgot the bravery of their local hero, Tefik Çanga, and named the school after him. Whether his friend gave any names under torture isn't known, but soon afterwards Sali's father Hasan was arrested and put on a train to a concentration camp in Germany. Many miles from Ferizaj, Hasan managed to escape by jumping from the moving train as it passed through Croatia. He made his way back to the Partisans, who gave him a white horse so he could work for them between the towns of Kukes and Gjakove. Sali said his father told him later that he was heartbroken when his white horse was wounded and he had to put down his close companion.

After school, Sali went to college to study economics and accountancy – and to form a pop group. It was the era of the Beatles and the Rolling Stones, and their records were as popular in Kosovo as in the rest of the world. As he could play the guitar, Sali spent the evening playing pop songs in his group, which he called the Illyrians, after the Roman name for Albania and the surrounding area. During the day, he studied and later worked in the accounts department at the furniture factory, one of the town's two main industries, the other being the production of oil from olives and sunflowers.

There were four in the band: Sali was bass guitar and soloist, the drummer, "the best in the college", was a Serbian, while two of Sali's cousins were lead guitarist and guitarist. Their manager was their economics and politics lecturer. There were two advantages for the group: first, the manager got them concerts at the college and in the town, and second, he always gave them good exam marks. They were going to be called the Blue Stars, and each had a blue star tattoo on their arm, which Sali still has today – but they decided instead to go for the Illyrians and wore Beatles T-shirts.

However, the young accountant got bored with Kosovo and the furniture factory, and in spring 1972 he decided to seek fame and fortune in Australia. To do that he had to attend an interview at their embassy, and the nearest one was in Vienna. He set off on the 1,000-kilometre journey with hardly any money and just one set of clothes, a pair of white trousers and a flowery silk shirt, as the Flower Power movement, the peaceful protest against the Vietnam War that began in America in the late 1960s, had reached as far as Kosovo.

Austria's capital was an important turning point for the 24-year-old Kosovan. There he found romance and God, in that order. He arrived at the Australian Embassy and was about to be ushered back onto the streets when he produced an official letter from the Ambassador. By chance, the Ambassador's wife was in the office and she took pity on the young Yugoslav, as she had been born in Bosnia. When she learnt he had nowhere to stay she offered him the spare room at their house, "for a couple of days". "I couldn't believe it," recalled Sali. "Here I was, a poor Kosovan, eating in the Ambassador's house, mixing with posh people and planning to emigrate to Australia."

There he met the Ambassador's son and daughter, and as his stay became more permanent, so did his friendship with their daughter. They started planning a future together. The couple talked of getting married, going to Australia, and running a chicken business which her family owned just outside Canberra.

Soon after the wedding discussions, Sali was walking through Vienna when he came across an open-air Christian meeting in the Prater, one of the city's most famous landmarks. With a funfair and a big wheel, it had gained a reputation as the place to meet, where lovers came on secret dates, where great composers performed and where poets and writers found inspiration. It was also the meeting place for the increasing numbers of illegal immigrants who had escaped to the West from Communist countries behind the Iron Curtain such as Russia, East Germany, Poland, Hungary, Romania, Bulgaria, Czechoslovakia, and Yugoslavia.

When Christians decided to try to help these people, they started an hour-long Sunday afternoon open-air service near the funfair in English, German, and Serbo-Croat. Sali was intrigued to hear songs in Serbo-Croat, a language he recognized, so he went over to find out more. Barbara Jamieson, a worker with ECM, started talking to him and invited him to go to church.

It was amazing that Barbara had ended up in Vienna doing street evangelism, as she was a qualified nurse and midwife. She was born in Bridlington, East Yorkshire, in 1934, but her father John, a fisherman, decided it was safer to move to the Shetland Islands when the Second World War broke out in 1939. He was right: a few months after they left, a German bomb landed on their house in Bridlington and badly damaged it.

After being converted at a Billy Graham rally, then training as a nurse, Barbara subsequently gave up nursing and joined ECM, eventually going out to Vienna.

She said she remembered Sali as "a very frightened young man who was very timid and always appeared very apprehensive". But he did turn up at the recently-formed evangelical church the following Sunday, where he was amazed to hear the pastor, Misko Horvatek, who was working with ECM, talking about how Jesus had healed the blind man Bartimaeus. After the service, he was even more surprised when he went to the back of the church and flicked open a copy of St John's Gospel. There on the first page was a picture of Jesus and the lamb. It was the one he had seen as a two-and-a-half-year-old behind the altar at Letnica. "I couldn't believe I saw the same picture," said Sali. "I began to wonder if God wasn't talking to me, and if Christianity wasn't true after all."

After a few weeks, and becoming more intrigued about this Jesus, he went to talk to the pastor, who said, "Do you believe in Jesus, the Son of God, who was born of the Virgin Mary?"

Sali nodded. The pastor then asked, "Do you believe Jesus came to earth, doing good and healing people?"

Again, Sali said yes, and so he asked a third question: "Do you believe Jesus died on the cross for you?" Sali nodded, and the pastor said all he then needed to do was acknowledge that with a prayer.

That evening, 14 August 1972, Sali went to the pastor's house and together with him, the pastor's wife, and their three children, he prayed. "I had been healed of my own blindness, and now I was healed of my spiritual blindness," said Sali. "I felt different; I had an overwhelming peace in my life."

He wasn't the only one to feel different – his girlfriend and his own family did as well. His view of Australia changed: instead he wanted to stay with his new church friends in Vienna, and to this day he has never been to Australia. His girlfriend said that in that case they would have to say goodbye. Sali had the difficult job of going to the embassy to see the official overseeing his emigration papers and to ask him to withdraw his application for Australia. The official was the Ambassador, who had nearly become Sali's father-in-law.

His real father took an even dimmer view of his son's news of becoming a Christian. Don't ever bother coming home, was his reply. Previously Sali had hardly ever bothered to write home. Now for the first time he felt he should write to his parents regularly, although for a long time he never heard anything back. Two years later Sali was walking through Vienna when a man who looked just like his father walked past him. Sali looked again and to his amazement realized it really was his father.

"Daddy, it's me!" shouted Sali.

His father turned and said, "I was looking for a person in black garments and a beard."

He thought his son had become an Orthodox priest, and had travelled the 1,000-kilometre journey to check that he was all right. Although it wasn't an emotional reunion, they enjoyed a couple of days together before his father returned to Kosovo without saying anything about the future, or so Sali thought. But the next time he went to church, the pastor told him he had been given a message from Sali's father that said, "You can tell my son he can come home now."

Sali, who still had hardly any clothes, had managed to find a bed in a hostel. He heard that a steel components factory was looking for workers, so he put on his white trousers and silk flowered shirt and went to meet the manager, who took pity on him as he could not speak any German. Sali said he would do any job, so he was told to report next day at 9 a.m. The manager was surprised to see him arrive in the same white trousers and silk flowered shirt, and said he was now a cleaner. It wasn't many minutes before his precious white trousers turned black in the steel works, but at least he was earning some money, so he could afford to buy some new clothes.

The manager was impressed by Sali's work commitment and it wasn't long before he trained him to be an engineering worker, which meant Sali's salary doubled overnight. His new-found wealth coincided with the time the church was looking for a new car. Sali had always wanted his own car, and he thought the obvious solution was to buy one and let the church use it when he didn't need it. He went to the local garage and there saw the car of his dreams. Even though he hadn't yet passed his driving test he drove it home to show his friend Branko Tihojevic, who was teaching him to drive, and also his pastor, Mishko, what he had bought.

They couldn't believe their eyes. "We can't have that car – you will have to take it back immediately," spluttered Misko.

Sali had bought a bright red Ford Mustang, a huge American car, which he had seen Elvis Presley driving in the film *Viva Las Vegas*. They took Sali back to the garage, where Misko explained the problem to a bemused car salesman. They returned with a much smaller and a much more sober-coloured Ford car. But Sali continued to like flashy cars. When a few months later an Australian volunteer with ECM offered to drive him home to see his family for a few days, Sali couldn't resist the idea of being driven in an open-top red MG. However, he had second thoughts as they sped south: twice the police stopped them for speeding.

News about Sali coming home spread through his family and friends, and they all wanted to meet him, having heard he had changed – and Sali certainly made an entrance, arriving in a red sports car. Dozens crowded into the family home to talk to him, and many didn't leave until 3 a.m., including the local priest, who said accusingly, "You have changed religion."

"No," replied Sali, "religion has changed me."

His outlook was certainly different and his attitude had become more caring, something that his friends and family, particularly his father, noticed.

When he returned to Vienna there was a letter waiting for him from the Billy Graham Organization, inviting him to a convention in Geneva.

"Why are they inviting me? I don't speak English. I would be wasting my time," he complained to his pastor.

"Perhaps they invited you because you are the only Albanian believer they know," he replied.

Why don't the Albanian people know God? Sali wondered. Suddenly he realized that perhaps God was calling him to serve his people in Albania. But how could he go to Albania, a closed country? Even though he could speak Albanian, he was a Kosovan, and they couldn't get into Albania. Then he remembered the story of the paralysed man in the Bible. His four friends could not see Jesus because of the crowds blocking the door, so they went up the outside steps and let him in from above through the roof.

If he couldn't get into Albania because the doors were shut, why not go in from above – with radio messages? But how could he do that?

By now, Sali and his friend Branko were fully involved with helping the ECM workers at the church. One day the ECM staff asked Sali and Branko if they would like to go to Bible college in Britain, sponsored by the mission. They would spend the first year at the ECM headquarters in Heightside, Rawtenstall, and then go to the Lebanon Bible College in Berwick-upon-Tweed.

They jumped at the chance, and just before Sali left Vienna he was asked to take a dozen radio scripts to ECM. A Yugoslav Christian in Peja, Simo Ralevic, had shown interest in the radio work, and ECM asked him to write a dozen scripts as a trial. Simo had helped Pastor Mishko Horvatek to come to faith, who in turn helped Sali become a Christian. Then Simo became a friend of Sali and lent him Christian books, so when he heard Sali was coming to ECM in England he entrusted him with the radio scripts.

Three important events happened the day Sali arrived in England on Wednesday 14 November 1973. First, the whole country was celebrating as Princess Anne married Captain Mark Phillips; second, it was Sali's first visit to England; third, and sadly, it was the day Alfred Andoni, who had worked for the BBC World Service, died.

When in 1967 Albania declared itself an atheistic country, ECM general director the Reverend Stuart Harris was praying for a way to get the Christian message into Albania by radio. ECM already had a radio studio, because it was recording messages for its work in Italy, but he needed someone who could speak Albanian and who lived in England. In July 1968, Stuart heard the BBC was cutting back on its foreign services and was axing a number of jobs, including Alfred Andoni's job on the Albania desk. Alfred was Albanian, married to an Englishwoman, and lived in London, where he worked part-time for the BBC in its Albanian broadcasts and part-time for British intelligence. Alfred would write and read news in Albanian for the BBC, and listened to all possible broadcasts from Albania to gather whatever information he could about what was going on inside the closed country.

Stuart offered to pay Alfred to translate messages from English into Albanian. Alfred went to the studios of WEC's Radio Worldwide, a Christian radio station based in south London, to record his messages, which were sent to Heightside's technical expert, who then forwarded them to Monte Carlo so they could be beamed into Albania. The first time they went to record the programme, the Christians said, "We will start with a prayer." "Why?" asked Alfred. The Christians explained that they were committing the programmes to God. Five years later, Alfred asked to meet Stuart in London. When Stuart asked him what the problem was, Alfred said it was his heart, and he now wanted to become a believer. They prayed together, and to show how serious Alfred was about becoming a Christian, he said to Stuart afterwards, "I have made a *besa*" (an Albanian word meaning a code of honour, which he would not break). Alfred was probably the first person converted by the Albanian radio programme, and it was also probably the first time a radio presenter had been converted by his own programme.

The radio staff were wondering where they were going to find another Albanian speaker, when in walked Sali – complete with twelve Albanian radio scripts.

The next day a nervous Sali began work, and over the next few months he translated other scripts written by ECM staff for the programme. Easter Sunday 1974 was a notable day for Sali, as it was the first time he wrote and broadcast his own message.

For twenty-years from November 1973 Sali faithfully broadcast the Christian message, not even knowing if a single person in Albania was listening to Luan Mateu's *Way of Peace* programmes. They were a mixture of Bible readings and studies, evangelistic messages, children's Bible stories and practical Christian teaching, including how to hold communion services in secret. He broadcast under the name Luan Mateu to protect his identity and because it would appeal to all Albanians, Luan being a Muslim name and Mateu a Roman Catholic one.

Little did Sali know then that there were many secret listeners in Albania itself, including a top government official, army officer Berti, and many adults and children, so justifying the faith of the radio staff, and particularly Dr Paul Freed, who had set up Trans World Radio all those years ago. At least he knew he had some Albanian fans who were tuning in to his programme in Kosovo. One of Sali's biggest fans was his dad, who told everyone, "Listen to my son; he is speaking on the radio from England." His father and one of Sali's brothers were so enthusiastic that they gave out many posters about the programme throughout the town. However, some were handed to the local police. That was to have serious repercussions for Sali when he returned home a few years later.

Members inside The Way of Peace Church.

Bedrija Manaj, who helps with the prayer meeting at The Way of Peace Church, sorting food boxes as part of the church's social work.

The men's fellowship at the Way of Peace Church with John Butterworth (right, seated) and Berti Dosti (left).

Berti used to put a headset on to listen secretly to Trans World Radio when he was a captain in the army. Now as a pastor, he puts on the headset every week to preach the gospel to Albanians via radio. Trans World Radio had helped an Albanian Christian organisation, Waves of the Gospel, to set up Radio 7 in Tirana and Berti is chairman of the board.

Berti leading a march during his time in the Albanian army.

Berti with his wife, Tatjana, in 1986.

Berti was presented with the Urdhri i Sherbimit Ushtarak te Klasit III, Albania's third highest military medal, on July 8, 1986. The citation said the medal was for "distinguished work in organisation and leadership in the military base where he served and attaining very high achievements of practice with his fellow soldiers."

One of the million pill boxes used to defend Albania during the rule of Enver Hoxha.

Berti's friend from schooldays, Ladi, outside his shop. Ladi continued to play an important part in Berti's life and the life of the church.

Sali Rahmani broadcast a Christian message by radio to Albania for twenty years. For the first eighteen years, he never had a letter back from Albania to prove anyone was listening.

Berti and Tatjana pictured with their two children, Alta and Dorian, at the summer camp in Vlore in July 1993.

Stephen and Tabita Bell with their three children Sheona, Joshua and Benjamin. Stephen spent five years learning Albanian at Pristina University before entering the country, and was one of the ECM workers who, along with Tabita, worked with the growing Albanian church.

The outside of the Victory School. Lessons started in 1997, on the first floor of a believer's house, before moving to the present building as the school grew.

Berti Dosti in his office as principal of the Victory School.

The outside of the Way of Peace Church, which is now located at the back of the Victory School.

Pastor Berti Dosti leads the worship at The Way of Peace Church, Lushnje.

Chapter 11

WE KNOW YOU ARE A CIA SPY

Sali had enjoyed his two years at Bible college in Berwick-upon-Tweed, but one question was troubling him. Should he marry a college girl he had become very friendly with: Helen McGinley, a Glaswegian Christian? She was very involved with Bible Centred Ministries International, a group dedicated to reaching children and developing churches worldwide, and she might soon go abroad, in which case he would never see her again. But Sali didn't know what he would be doing when he finished college. When ECM invited Sali to move to Munich to work alongside another of their workers, Tom Lewis, he decided to accept that offer and to ask Helen to marry him.

On 26 June 1976, which would later turn out to be a very auspicious date, they were married at Mosspark Baptist Church in Glasgow. After a three-day honeymoon in Berwick-upon-Tweed, the newly married couple drove out to Munich with their best man, Branko Tihojevic, to begin their new ministry.

For the next four years, Sali threw himself into his work with overseas workers, while he continued to send his Christian tapes back to Rawtenstall to be broadcast into Albania via Monte Carlo. He lived in a block of flats and recorded the programmes in the bedroom. However, he would try to work when the lift wasn't being used, as it was so noisy that it could be heard on his tapes. At first he produced one programme a week, then it grew to two and finally three nights a week. When an American Southern Baptist later donated £40,000, Trans World Radio was able to broadcast seven nights a week.

Every Friday afternoon Sali used to go down to Munich railway station. The 5:17 train to Thessalonica was the one on which Yugoslavs and Kosovar Albanians would return home, and Sali was given permission by the railway authorities to preach in the station foyer, to give out free literature, and to sell Bibles.

Usually he had no problems at all, but one day while preaching he noticed two well-built men in suits watching him suspiciously. He thought nothing more about it and continued giving his Christian message. As he finished and turned his back, ready to move through to the railway platform to give out his literature, the two men suddenly grabbed him and frogmarched him to a nearby toilet cubicle. "You are in big trouble," one of them said to him. "I was so shocked I couldn't say anything at first," Sali recalled. "What the two didn't realize was that as they spoke in Serbo-Croat, I could understand everything they were saying."

He realized that they were planning to drug him and then take him back secretly to Yugoslavia. They were dragging him into the toilet when he saw a German police officer and managed to shout for help in German. As the police officer came over, the two abductors let go of Sali and melted into the crowd. Sali was shaken by this incident. However, as the weeks went by he forgot about it and settled back into family and church life.

Sali and Helen's first daughter was born and was named Hanusha after her grandmother – although the daughter had the Albanian spelling while her grandmother's name was the Turkish Muslim spelling. Later Sali and Helen had two sons, Simon and Luan, the latter named after his father's radio persona. In 1980 they left Munich and moved to Vienna to work in the ECM offices. Sali believed that Albania would open its borders to visitors and he wanted to prepare for that day, which he reckoned would be around 1994 (he was actually four years late). In Vienna, Sali continued with his radio broadcasting, but all the time the question continued to nag him: was anyone listening?

In April 1983 he decided to combine a trip home to Kosovo to see his parents with an exploratory visit into the nearby villages and towns to find if there were any listeners to his programme there. His colleagues at ECM weren't too keen on the idea, but Sali persuaded them to let him go, and he and a radio operator and technician, Peter Harrison, set off to Ferizaj, Kosovo, in a rusty old Renault.

Peter, who was born in Harrow in 1944, the third of four brothers, had become a Christian when he was a teenager at Marlow Baptist Church. After leaving school at sixteen, he became an apprentice instrument maker at Courtaulds. Later he was challenged to go to All Nations Missionary College.

After Bible college, Peter joined ECM in January 1970 as a probationary missionary, and on the second day at the Foreign Missions Club in London, where he was living, he met a Swiss au pair girl, Susi, and they married in October 1973. Later they moved to Vienna, where Peter, who had now become interested in radio work, prepared the tapes to send to Trans World Radio so they could beam Sali's message into Albania.

Everything went well until Peter and Sali came to the Slovenian border. There they were searched thoroughly and even their shoes were X-rayed. "They stripped the vehicle so thoroughly they took the wheels off," recalled Peter. "Then they put the car over a pit and checked the underneath, even pointing out things that the Austrian mechanics had missed in the MOT inspection."

Sali told Peter to return to Vienna and said he would make his own way to Ferizaj. "I told him I am not leaving Yugoslavia without him," said Peter. "I knew as long as I was there, the authorities would think twice about doing anything to Sali." When Sali heard this, he burst into tears. As Peter was a British passport holder, the customs officials treated him very leniently. However, they told Sali not to tell Peter anything. But Sali replied, "He is my friend." This worried them because in Albanian culture there is always a strong bond between friends.

Sali, as a Yugoslav national, bore the brunt of the questions. He was interrogated in a room on his own at the customs post for five hours and his passport was taken from him. They asked him, What are you doing in Vienna? Who are you working for? Why are you forcibly propagating the Christian gospel? Sali patiently explained that he was a missionary and all he was doing was presenting the Christian message. Then they asked him, Why are you working for Radio Free Europe? This was an American radio station which had broadcast from Munich to the USSR and Eastern Europe during the Cold War to counteract the Communist propaganda. Until 1972, the American spy network, the Central Intelligence Agency, had funded it, and the Russians had tried unsuccessfully to jam the broadcasts.

While in Munich, Sali lived very close to the Radio Free Europe studios and he had been invited to do some broadcasting. He was tempted, but after talking it through with ECM he decided against it. Now he could confidently tell the officials that they were wrong: he had never worked for Radio Free Europe. After five hours of questioning and document-checking, Sali and Peter were allowed to continue to Ferizaj. However, there was one condition – Sali would have to stay at his parents' house for the whole month, and the police would call for him every day and escort him to the police station. They had wanted to keep Sali in a police station cell, but they were all full.

What had been a relatively simple questioning at the border turned into a more sinister one at Ferizaj. The first morning, Sali was taken to a plush office in the police station with three leather chairs, a black shiny table, and a tatty, rickety, wooden chair. He was told to sit on the old chair while three police officials settled down into the leather chairs. Straightaway Sali had two shocks.

First, one of the police officers was a Kosovar Albanian whom he knew a little, as he had been at college with his brother. Even worse, Sali's father, when he was a town official, had bought this Kosovar Albanian's father some electricity when he was in desperate need. Second, they knew everything about his life – from his schooldays to his Christian conversion in Vienna, from his studies in England to his work in Munich, and, of course, his radio work as Luan Mateu. They even knew about his invitation to Switzerland for a few days one Christmas to preach to a group of forty-one Yugoslavs, of whom thirty-eight were Kosovar Albanians.

It suddenly dawned on Sali that the incident in Munich when the two men had nearly dragged him into a toilet cubicle was not an isolated one; it was part of a continuing surveillance on him. What he didn't realize until later was that Albanian officials had written to the authorities in Kosovo to say they had been watching Sali Rahmani for a long time. However, Sali didn't know anything about that as the questions began.

"What is this radio programme, The Way of Peace? What

peace are you bringing?"

They went through every aspect of his life for the whole day, every day. He was not given any food and had only one drink until he returned to his parents' house in the evening.

At this time, there were tensions between the Kosovar Albanians and the Serbs and the Yugoslav authorities, and the situation was beginning to boil over, with protests and even bomb attacks.

"Rahmani," the three interrogators went on, "this religious work is just a cover for your political objectives. You are trying to foment unrest in different parts of Europe against the Yugoslav government."

A few months earlier, there had been an attack in Stuttgart in which a couple of bombs exploded, and Sali was accused of being behind that.

"You are working for intelligence agencies in Western Europe and America, aren't you? We know you are a CIA spy."

The questions went on day after day, and Sali kept answering that he was a missionary doing God's work, and denying any political motives or links to the CIA. Even his mother and father were questioned, but the police couldn't find any evidence to implicate Sali. However, as a couple of weeks passed by, Sali began to get worried, because no one knew what had happened to him. His wife Helen and his children would be concerned, because they would soon be preparing to go to an ECM conference in Germany and they had had no news about him.

After a couple of weeks Peter decided to take a chance, leave Sali's parents' house, and go to the post office to ring his wife. It was risky, because there was a queue for phones and everyone could hear what was being said – and it was presumably passed on to the police. Still, Peter managed to get through and asked his wife to give a message to Sali's wife Helen and ECM's Eastern European director Tom Lewis. "I wasn't worried myself about what was going on, but I thought it would be more disconcerting for my wife not knowing what was happening," said Peter, who also contacted Sali's friend Simo Ralevic, from Peja. Simo managed to meet and encourage Sali, for which he was very grateful.

Each day Sali prayed that he would be able to tell his story of why he had become a Christian, but he was never allowed to. "You are trying to convert us," they sneered whenever Sali mentioned his faith. "It's not me but God who will convert you," Sali would reply.

The interrogators, meanwhile, changed their tactics and decided to try the nice approach. One day only the Kosovar Albanian turned up, and he was much softer.

"I am proud of you," he began. "Your family were very kind to our family. I want you to come and work in Kosovo: I can get you a job. First, you have to admit to me that you were involved in these bomb attacks. At the moment your life is in a mess."

Sali replied, "As a Christian, I can't tell you a lie just to please you."

The interrogator got up from his chair and hit Sali so hard across his face that he fell back in his ramshackle chair. He found himself sprawled across the floor, with the chair in pieces and the hot coffee he had been drinking all over his face.

When the two Serbian interrogators arrived in the room, they were told that Sali had grabbed the chair and begun to attack the Kosovar Albanian, who naturally had to defend himself. In turn, they hit Sali and warned him they were preparing to send him to the High Court in Belgrade, where he would face at least twenty-two years in jail.

The next session became even nastier, as they said they had received information that Sali's wife Helen had left him and that she and their children had gone to live with her father in Scotland. Sali, however, knew that they were due to go to the ECM conference in Germany. They continually accused Sali of propagating the Christian message, mostly through his radio work. But one day they produced a plastic bag with an Albanian John's Gospel in it, plus a large straw to keep the bag afloat, some chewing gum, and Christian literature on which there were Sali's contact details.

What do you know about these? demanded his interrogators. Sali knew about them, but very wisely he had asked the Christians involved not to tell him too many details. Now he was glad he had been careful. Some Christians had approached him with an imaginative scheme to get the Christian message into Albania. This group had filled 1,000 plastic bags and dropped them into the 335-kilometre-long River Drin in Kosovo to float downstream into Albania.

Another idea Sali knew of was much more foolhardy. Two Americans wanted to buy a huge stack of Sali's Albanian Christian literature. Their idea was to rent two planes, fly over Albania, and drop the literature by parachute. Fortunately, he talked the American pilots out of their outrageous plan, mainly on military grounds. He said that although the Albanian military was not the best in Europe, they still had enough equipment and training to shoot down two small planes in their airspace.

His interrogators refused to accept that Sali had not had anything to do with the unusual plastic bags mission, despite all his protestations. They told him that it in any case it had been a useless enterprise, since the authorities had fished all the plastic bags out of the river. So Sali was delighted when about ten years later on a visit to Christians in Krujé when one of them produced the plastic bag and Christian literature which he had found in the river and had read.

Meanwhile, Sali was wondering how he could convince the interrogators of his innocence, when one of them let slip that the plastic bags had been put into the river on Saturday 26 June 1976. Suddenly Sali shouted with delight. "I can prove it wasn't me. I had nothing to do with those plastic bags dropped into the river. I wasn't even in Kosovo on that day. I was a couple of thousand miles away," he added triumphantly. "I was in Glasgow – it was my wedding day!"

Peter's courage in making the phone calls had also paid dividends. Tom Lewis, who was a friend of Dr Ian Paisley, spoke to the Northern Ireland politician, who helped mobilize MPs and Foreign Office officials. Meanwhile, church leaders contacted the Baptist Union in Zagreb, who in turn wrote to the Yugoslav government.

Tom, who was born in Belfast in 1940, was taken as a 19-year-old to a Christian rally led by Dr Ian Paisley. Tom joined ECM officially in 1971, working firstly in Munich and then in Vienna when he served as ECM's Eastern European director from 1978 until 1990.

Meanwhile, at the ECM conference in Stuttgart they were praying for Sali every day. Tom decided to drive to Ferizaj to give Sali and Peter moral support – and the marriage certificate to show to the police. By the fourth week the interrogators relented and let Sali tell the story of his conversion. "You have just ten minutes," they told him. Sali spoke for one hour and fifteen minutes. His interrogators were visibly moved. The Kosovar Albanian told him, "I would wish our young people would be like you. If you need any help, please contact me." With that, he gave him a card with his direct office phone number. Within two days the interrogator returned to tell Sali, "I have very good news. I have your passport: you are free to leave."

When Sali returned home, there was only time for a quick farewell to his parents before racing off to the border. Tom knew of cases in which Christians had been released by the authorities and then, when they arrived at the border, customs officials had opened their cases and found drugs planted on them. But Tom wasn't worried about the journey. "I had done far more difficult trips into Eastern Europe previously, smuggling Bibles into Russia, Romania, Bulgaria, and Czechoslovakia," he said. Tom drove Sali straight to Vienna so that Peter could be reunited with his wife Susi, before taking them all to the ECM conference in Germany. One of those at the conference who had been praying for Sali's safety was Barbara Jamieson, who had first invited him to go to church in Vienna in 1972.

"It was like chapter 12 in the Book of Acts," said Sali. "Peter was arrested by King Herod, put in prison, and then miraculously delivered. He walked straight from prison into a prayer meeting. The same happened to me. I went straight from house arrest into meeting people who had been praying for me. It was very emotional."

Nevertheless, although Sali hadn't been able to try to track down any listeners on that visit, it didn't put him off trying twice again in the next three years – and each time he was arrested.

Two years later, he returned to his family home in Ferizaj. This time, the same Kosovar Albanian police officer who had questioned him the previous time interrogated him again. After four days he was released, and he bumped into his interrogator in the town. To show there were no hard feelings, Sali gave him the kilo of coffee he had brought with him from Vienna. "He was very grateful and moved by the gesture," said Sali.

This time he managed to travel and meet some of his listeners. His father Hasan insisted on accompanying his son. Whether it was for security reasons or because he was inquisitive, or both, Sali never found out. They went to a village just outside Prishtina and met a listener who had written letters to Sali and the radio station. Hasan was amazed by the reaction when a complete stranger greeted Sali as a friend and invited him to a meal in his house. The householder told Sali in front of everyone, "You are very welcome: you are part of our family, you are here with us every night." Later Hasan told his son, "Thank you: I enjoyed the visit very much."

After that Hasan, a former hardline Communist, changed. He never told Sali whether he had become a Christian, but he told his friends in his street, "God is my friend and I am his friend."

A year later, in 1986, Sali had to return home because his father had died. Again he was questioned, for two days, but this time it didn't matter. Because of the distance Sali had had to travel, he had arrived too late for the funeral anyway.

Chapter 12

THE TIMES THEY ARE A-CHANGIN'

1989 was the year when both Albania and Berti began to change. The leader of the Party of Labour (the Communist Party), Ramiz Alia, had tried to introduce a programme of cautious liberalization. But the people were impatient for change as they watched the Berlin Wall torn down that year and the old governments of Eastern Europe overthrown. When the Ceausescu regime in nearby Romania fell in December 1989, Ramiz Alia knew he had to speed up the reforms, even though the Foreign Minister defiantly declared, "What is happening in Eastern Europe has nothing to do with us." The press was freed and opposition newspapers were allowed for the first time, while opposition political parties began to form and the ban on contact with foreigners was removed. The following year the death penalty was abolished for most anti-state offences.[1]

However, these cautious changes did not satisfy the people, who were impatient for more radical ones. The authorities became nervous as rioting broke out all over the country, and they ordered the military to draw up a Rapid Defence Force to quell the riots and to protect public buildings such as town halls, schools, political offices, and hospitals from the mobs.

One of those the Defence Ministry called up first was Berti, who was sent to a special base at Kavaja at the end of 1989, ironically the scene of his greatest military achievement, where he had been presented with his top medal. While the units were in training, the political situation deteriorated further. In January 1990, thousands of Albanians fled to Greece, and crowds, mainly young people, seized many of the foreign embassies. Then there was the first students' protest on 8 December 1990, which started in Kavaja.

Tanks were stationed on the Albanian streets, and Berti's job, as communications chief at Kavaja, was to be the link between the soldiers in the tanks and his Commandant. Berti admitted that the soldiers were unhappy to be deployed against their own people, but they were told not to confront the protesters who wanted democracy, and to avoid trouble if possible. He said the situation became more tense when the Albanian government sent up soldiers from Skrapar, an area three hours to the south, which was still pro-Hoxha, to Kavaja, which was anti-Communist.

The protests on the streets continued throughout 1990 and into 1991, when on 21 February crowds pulled down the large statue of Enver Hoxha in the central square of Tirana. "That was the day Communism in Albania ended," said Berti.

The political situation was defused in the short term in March 1991, when the first democratic elections in Albania were held. The partially reformed Party of Labour won, mainly because many of the rural people didn't want change and couldn't see on TV what was happening in the rest of Europe. The new government lasted only two months: a three-week general strike in May forced its resignation and led to a national unity coalition government, including non-Communists.

With food riots and troubles everywhere, the new government

put the country on the highest military alert. Reservists were called up and the Rapid Defence Forces was deployed on the streets again, at the same time as the European Economic Community launched a major aid programme, Operation Pelican, overseen by the Italian army. Politicians went on TV to appeal for calm, accusing the students of being immature and asking the people whether they were prepared for an enemy invasion, which could happen now as the borders were open.

As Bill Hamilton wrote in his book, *Albania – Who Cares?*,

> By then the country was in economic chaos, its people queuing sometimes for hours just to get bread.
>
> To watch the excitement of children walking home with a loaf under each arm, you would have thought they were carrying bars of gold. At night, many of them were sent on to the streets by their parents to set rubbish alight to keep them warm. Firewood was fast running out.
>
> Along some country roads there was hardly a tree left standing, such was the desperation. The shops were empty – no meat, no fish, no coffee. At one stage, the entire railway network had to be closed down. The general manager feared a disaster. Railway sleepers were removed for fuel, and signalling wire was torn down by those who had thought of an innovative way of connecting electrical supplies from streetlights into their homes.
>
> Nearly 70 per cent of the adult population were out of work. There were no raw materials for the factories. Machines stood idle and resilience was wearing thin. One electrical worker trying to mend a severed cable was machine-gunned to death by an angry mob. Lethargy had set in, with Albanians losing the desire to work and becoming almost totally dependent on Western aid.[2]

Eventually a third election was held in March 1992 and the Democrats swept to power with more than 60 per cent of the vote. To show how desperate the situation was, a power failure in Tirana on election night meant the ballot papers were sorted by candlelight.

The next day more than 100,000 people filled Skenderbeu Square to celebrate the Democrats' victory, and cars drove triumphantly around the city centre until they ran out of fuel. It was the beginning of a new era as Albania came in from the cold after nearly fifty years of Stalinist isolation. The new president, 48-year-old cardiologist Sali Berisha, symbolized this by refusing to move into the Presidential Palace, deciding to stay instead with his family in their two-bedroomed flat on a rundown Tirana housing estate.

It was also the beginning of a new era for Berti. What he had seen on the streets of Kavaja had made him question his military role and his career. He had watched as soldiers used guns to fire over the crowds of people to frighten them. He had been convinced that no soldiers would ever fire, or to be ordered to fire, on their own people. However, their rules said that they had to protect the government at whatever cost, and if necessary with their lives. "I had loved my profession, but for the first time I began to rebel against the army. I hadn't joined to do this," he admitted.

He even challenged his superior officers about what was going on. Now Albanians knew there was no enemy about to attack them, they said there was no need to have so many military bases. In addition, the economic situation in Albania meant the military budget had to take its share of cutbacks. "When I went to the base there were twenty officers hanging around with nothing to do," said Berti. "I said to my commanding officers, 'What are we doing? We will become a lazy army.'"

The problem was that most of them thought it was impossible for them to find work if they left the army, whereas Berti knew he could. Previously, he had tuned in when he could to the Trans World Radio broadcasts and Luan Mateu's programme. However, with his move to the Rapid Defence Forces he began to listen more often, sometimes recording the programmes to listen to them again later. With the army becoming more disorganized, discipline breaking down everywhere, the government more relaxed, and Albanian liberation seemingly not far away, in 1991 Berti plucked up the courage to write to Trans World Radio.

By 1991 Berti knew his army career was ending, so he began planning for the future. At the same time, he met up again with his second cousin Tomorr Dosti, who used to come from Tirana to spend his summer holidays in Lushnjë with Berti. Now Tomorr, who was a customs officer at Rinas, Tirana's main airport, also ran a business, and he offered to lend Berti some money to open a kiosk.

Since Albania had begun to opens its borders in 1990, there was more money coming into the country, mainly from Albanians working abroad who wanted to help their relatives back home. In addition, Albanians, after years of austerity, were making up for lost time and were hungry for education and goods such as chocolates, sweets, chewing gum, cigarettes, and stationery. The more Berti thought about the idea of opening a kiosk, the more he liked it. He knew he couldn't go back to his previous career of repairing radios. He had spent so much time working on army radios that his knowledge of ordinary radios was out of date.

But a kiosk was an excellent business idea, and he knew the ideal location. Since he was still in the army he needed a partner to help him run it, but Berti thought immediately of someone who could help him. He went back to his old friend Ladi and his "adopted parents", Leksi and Liri. Ladi was delighted to join him, while his parents allowed them to put up a kiosk in their garden, on the corner of a busy junction. It went so well, with Ladi running it in the mornings and Berti looking after it when he had finished his army duties, that they soon expanded by selling groceries and staying open until 10 p.m. to provide coffee. Within eighteen months, Berti had repaid the loan to his cousin and there was enough money in the business for Ladi and Berti to buy a car.

Chapter 13

I THINK I RECOGNIZE YOUR VOICE, SAID THE GOVERNMENT OFFICIAL

Every radio presenter is always interested to know how many people are listening to his or her programme. However, to Sali Rahmani it was even more basic: Is anyone in Albania listening? It was a question which ECM had been trying to answer for years. The first people to try were Barbara Jamieson, who worked for ECM in Vienna, and Margaret Willan, who worked for ECM in Munich with the Eastern Europeans.

When in 1975 a Czech charter company advertised probably the first ever holiday to Albania, Barbara and Margaret couldn't resist going. However, even they were a little surprised when they met up with the rest of the group and found that most of the thirty-strong party were German Communists going to Albania to help build a railroad.

Their flight was uneventful until they tried to land at the airport in Tirana, Albania's equivalent of Heathrow in Britain, and found there were cows on the only runway. In addition, even though it was an airport, there were no other planes. "The only planes to use the airport were from Communist China, and they landed and took off only on Saturdays and Sundays," recalled Margaret.[1]

Border guards checked their cases and asked them three questions. “Have you any books against our government? Have you any bombs? Have you brought any foreign newspapers or periodicals in the country?” Their guide was a pharmacist from East Germany, who told them they couldn’t leave their hotel without his permission. “He had been brought back home so he could translate for the Germans,” explained Margaret. The two women enjoyed their ten-day holiday and had a good tour of the whole country. However, what stood out for them was the lack of traffic, particularly cars. “Members of the diplomatic corps had cars, but most people travelled by bus, lorry, ox-cart, donkey, or bicycle,” said Margaret. In the small towns and villages they noted that some people had small transistor radios. “We saw a group of men had placed one in a red cover under a black umbrella and were sitting round it, listening,” said Margaret. “These transistors provided for the reception of long and medium wave bands. The opportunities we had to switch on sets with short wave bands in the hotels proved to us the bands were very congested and there was much jamming.” Radios were expensive. One model with three wave bands which they saw in a shop was priced at 800 lek, which was more than a month’s wages, and for some people almost double their wages.

Although they didn’t find any listeners to Trans World Radio, they did discover the programmes were going out at the wrong time, when workers were changing shifts. When they returned home, they reported this to Sali Rahmani and the radio team changed the time to beam the programmes into Albania.

Sali knew that the change of time had made a difference in other places. When he went back home to Kosovo in the 1980s and to other parts of Europe, he found there were listeners. He had first-hand proof of that: one of them was now working for him. Since 1987, Rifat Buzuku, a professional boxer, had tuned in to Sali's programme from Kosovo and when he moved to Dortmund, Germany, he continued listening. He came to England to meet Sali, was converted, and was then invited to work for ECM in Vienna. Rifat sent literature to listeners, replied to their letters, translated tapes, and sometimes even wrote his own scripts, as well as going to Bible school in Austria. "Rifat was a great help and also did some of the tapes for Sali's programme," recalled Peter Harrison.

Were there listeners in Albania itself? When ECM held its 1991 conference in Corfu, the Greek island that is only a few kilometres from Albania, the temptation to go there on a day trip was too much for Sali. There was a two-hour ferry crossing leaving Corfu in the morning and returning from Sarande in Albania in the afternoon. As no visas were needed, he persuaded ECM director David Clark and twenty-eight other conference delegates to join him.

The main reason tourists go to Sarande is to visit Butrint. Even though it is a UNESCO World Heritage site, it is still one of the great but largely unknown archaeological sites of the eastern Mediterranean. The 1,100-acre site was probably founded when King Priam's son Helenus came from Troy and married Andromache. The story of the couple inspired the seventeenth-century French dramatist Jean Racine to write his classical tragedy *Andromache*, which is set there. This former Greek colony and later Roman town with an amphitheatre seating 5,000 was mentioned in Virgil's *Aeneid* and the *Letters of Cicero*. Its first bishop was consecrated in AD 451.[2]

That autumn in 1991 Sarande probably had its most unusual tourist invasion, as thirty Western Christians arrived, singing and giving out literature and copies of John's Gospel in Albanian. "We didn't know what to expect," said David, "but we were inundated with crowds of people, including soldiers wanting to see who we were, to take our gifts, and to try out their English on us."

After time in the attractive port and seaside town of Sarande, with its pleasant small beach, fringed with palm trees, the group moved on to Gjirokastër, Enver Hoxha's birthplace. Gjirokastër is also a UNESCO World Heritage city, famous for its Ottoman buildings, particularly its thirteenth-century citadel. While the ECM members were walking up to the citadel, they met some teenage girls, who followed them and wanted to practise their English.

"Have you heard of God and Jesus Christ?" asked David.

"We have heard of God, but who is Jesus Christ?" they replied.

David was used to forbidden countries. His parents had been missionaries in China, and when his mother was pregnant with him they had had to flee from Chongqing in Sichuan Province in Western China when there was a clampdown on missionaries. "I tell people I have a label on me saying 'Made in China'," he would say. After a career as an engineer, he joined ECM as a voluntary area representative in 1975 before becoming British director in 1983 and later Western Europe director. In 1993 he succeeded Jack Murray as leader of ECM International.

Despite Sali's best efforts, they didn't find one listener that day. It would be another five months before Sali found some listeners in a most unexpected place, when he returned to Albania for a week in September, and under unusual circumstances.

In autumn 1991 Dr Janet Goodall had just retired after a successful career as consultant paediatrician in North Staffordshire when she had a phone call from Ron Newby, a social worker whom she had known when he worked with the Children's Society in the West Midlands.

When Ron retired, he was asked in 1983 to visit war-torn Uganda in the aftermath of Idi Amin's regime, and he was so moved by the desperate plight of the children there that he set up Global Care, a British-registered international Christian charity. The second country the charity helped was Romania, after Ron had visited the orphanages there. However, when he later saw TV pictures of ships overladen with Albanians fleeing to Italy, and naked, emaciated children who were held in desperate conditions in barren institutions, he knew that had to be the third country the charity would help. Ron realized he needed a paediatrician to take with him, so he rang Dr Goodall. "It was September 1991," recalled Janet, "and Ron was ready to travel the next week. The fact that we had no visas, no local currency, and no knowledge of the language did not deter him. He was still prepared to go, even when he didn't receive any answers to his faxes explaining our intentions to some of the government ministries."

Although Janet had agreed to accompany Ron, she was slightly concerned by the lack of planning. However, she was relieved when just a few days before they were due to fly Ron told her that he had stumbled across an Albanian-speaking Christian, Sali Rahmani, who had agreed to accompany them. Midway through the flight Janet's heart sank when she learned that her interpreter was on the Albanian government's blacklist because of his Christian activities. "We therefore set off without visas and a 'suspicious character', not knowing whether we would all three be clapped into jail on arrival," said Janet later.

However, there was no chance of Sali slipping unnoticed into the country. As he left the plane and walked over to the terminal, he was so emotional at being in Albania that, in Papal fashion, he fell on his knees, kissed the tarmac, and shouted "Hallelujah" in front of bemused passengers and airline staff.

Sali was very happy to be in Albania, but he was nervous about what sort of reception he would get.

There were two surprises awaiting them in the arrivals hall. First, the officials allowed them into the country with the minimum of fuss, and second, there was a group of Albanian Christians to greet them and take the visitors by taxi into Tirana. At the time, no private cars were allowed, and there were only a few taxis on the deserted roads of the capital, a situation that was to change dramatically within a few years when Tirana's streets, like those of so many big cities, became choked with cars.

The Christians had arranged for the three to stay with a young man, Petro, who had agreed to open his flat to them. Janet, who had the settee in the dining room, said she was amazed to see the walls lined with bookshelves full of volumes of Shakespeare translated into Albanian. She learnt later that Petro's father was at one time a language professor at Tirana University, while his evangelical grandfather had helped to bring back the Albanian language and the gospel to the country. Petro said his grandfather had been invited to dinner by members of the Greek Orthodox Church "to explain his beliefs" and had died shortly afterwards. Petro was convinced he was poisoned, but whether it was that or natural food poisoning was never proved.

Petro wanted to follow his father into the academic world, but when he was younger, Albanians were told where they were going and what job they would be doing. Petro had to train as an electrical engineer, although Janet was not totally convinced by his skills when she saw the bare trailing wires in the bathroom. He was, however, a kind and generous host, getting up early to go to market to get cheese and bread for his visitors.

The next day, Janet, Sali, and Ron set off to try to meet a deputy minister of foreign affairs with whom Ron had been corresponding. They were invited into the office of Dr Maksim Bozo, who fished Ron's fax out of his shirt pocket and said that he had been expecting them, even though he had never replied to it. Dr Bozo, who Janet was delighted to learn was a paediatrician like herself, took them into a beautiful room with a sumptuous carpet. Over coffee, he introduced them to the Minister of Foreign Affairs. In the room were about a dozen people, the equivalent of Britain's senior civil servants, as Sali began translating for Ron and Janet and explaining why they had come.

Sali was slightly unnerved by a very senior person sitting opposite him who kept looking at him and smiling while he was talking. When there was a break in the meeting the civil servant sidled up to Sali and asked him, "What is your job?"

"I am a missionary: I preach the gospel," replied Sali.

"Have you spoken on the radio? I think I recognize your voice," he continued. Sali admitted he had.

"Is your name Luan Mateu?" he asked again. When Sali replied it was his radio name, the civil servant embraced him.

"I am so glad to see you," he said. The official told how he had been ordered by the Albanian government to monitor the radio programmes, which he did. He later told his bosses that there was nothing to worry about from the broadcasts, but he continued to listen.

"Something has happened to me, thanks to your radio

programme," he said.

When they reassembled after coffee, the minister said in front of everyone, "I gather you have a radio name and a real name, but that doesn't matter. We are glad you have a heart for your country and we welcome you and thank you for your visit, even though I gather you have already been visiting us for a long time, in fact every night."

The visit was such a success that Dr Bozo took Janet, Sali, and Ron in his ministry car, plus chauffeur, to visit paediatric institutions around the country. Janet recalled that they spent the days on visits with Dr Bozo and the evenings following the local custom of gathering in the city squares or parks, where parents and their children, dressed in their best clothes, promenaded or sat chatting in groups. It was all very friendly and the three foreigners quickly became the focal point for Albanians who wanted to practise their English. More importantly, they wanted to know why Sali had come. "As he explained about his missionary radio work," said Janet, "it was like New Testament times when the Apostles first took the good news around the Mediterranean. Sali was soon engulfed in the crowd, delighted to be able to explain in person what he had so far only been able to share by radio. In the end, Ron, who was quite a large person in build, had to fish Sali, who was of quite small build, out of the eager throng, as he was worried his evangelist might get trampled on."

On the Saturday evening Sali spoke at a big evangelistic meeting in one of Tirana's main halls. Eleven young people became Christians, and they were baptized on Sunday afternoon in the nearby lake.

The Bozos insisted on inviting Janet, Sali, and Ron to their home for a meal. Here they learned life was still tough, even if you were a deputy minister's wife. Dr Bozo's wife Monda said she had to get up during the night, while there was a reasonably good water supply, to fill the bath for all their needs next day before the supply failed. There were frequent electricity cuts and food supplies were very limited, with many bare shelves. Janet said she was amazed one day when she went shopping and watched Monda looking for the best prices for parsley. The standard wage for all employees was $20 a month, whatever your rank in the government, so even a deputy minister's wife had to be careful with the household budget.

After a few days, Sali returned home as planned. However, Dr Bozo continued the tour, this time bringing along his eighteen-year-old daughter Evis as interpreter. She had wanted to learn English at school but had been refused because, she was told, "It is the language of spies." But this hadn't put her off, and she had got up at 5 a.m. every day for five years to learn English for two hours before going to school. Her tutors were an old-fashioned textbook belonging to her parents, and the BBC World Service. The whole family would have been in big trouble had she been discovered, but she succeeded so well that she impressed her visitors with her accent and vocabulary – even though they were the first English people she had met.

Although she was Albanian, even Evis was shocked by the awful places where her father took them. "It was like going back to the days of Dickens," said Janet, "although the institutionalized children had little hope of asking for more. The thin gruel that was their staple diet clearly did not nourish them. Although I became all too familiar with malnutrition when I worked in Uganda, I had never ever seen such emaciated white children en masse in Europe."

The infants lay in rows at the bottom of cots, jammed together in otherwise bare, long white rooms and with not a toy in sight. "We found later in some of the better places," added Janet, "that aid had included toys, but these were locked away in cupboards 'in case the children broke them'." The general sensory deprivation had produced the characteristic signs described by Spitz and Bowlby in British orphanages in the early 1900s. The infants' eyes had an empty, unresponsive stare; the backs of their heads were bald, ceaselessly moving back and forth. "As we approached the toddlers' ward we could hear the creak of the cots before we went in. We found their occupants standing up, rocking back and forth, with no other form of available play. The few put into a playpen were listless and apathetic, unless they were strong enough to stand up and hang on to the side. Evis handed out Smarties, but the children did not know what to do with this unfamiliar confectionery."

Then the group went to the dystrophic unit, where infants who were failing to thrive went. "I noticed one of the carers with tears in her eyes as she observed our concern," said Janet. Most carers were poor themselves. In addition, should mothers wish to visit recently admitted children they were expected to bribe their way in to supplement the very poor pay of the attendants. Even a breast-feeding mother could not stay for longer than a week if her baby still failed to gain weight, Janet was told. Equipment was basic, with tin mugs often used rather than bottles, even for young babies.

If the institutions in Tirana were bad, they were far worse in the southern city of Berat, a beautiful historical site that has what many claim to be the finest large medieval citadel in the Balkans. There they were taken to the Befatrof, which means "the house of the foolish", a home for mentally handicapped children under the age of sixteen. Many of the children there were roaming about, clad in dirty and inadequate rags. "My abiding recollections of this place are of broken windows, bad smells, terribly battered iron bedsteads with badly chipped enamel, worn-out bedding, rusted and defunct radiators, and the doctor in charge telling us that half the sick children on his acute ward would die within a year," said Janet. Because Evis had started university that day, their interpreter was Dr Gazim Boçari, a professor of pharmacology, who told them his university laboratory was so devoid of materials that his days were spent concocting an ointment out of onions.

One girl who caught Janet's attention that day was a child of about seven who seemed to have no facial features at all, apart from grotesque, bloodshot eyes with scarred and retracted eyelids following severe burns. Her skin was dark and scaly and one of her hands was badly deformed, with flexed and fixed fingers. She was unnecessarily totally blind, her inability to blink having caused chronic infection of both eyes. When the little girl's mother had died, her father remarried and her stepmother could not stand the child's facial appearance, so she was put in the nearest institution at the age of three. She had been given no formal education and could not even count. Her condition was believed to have originated in a house fire, but even that was doubted, with village gossip saying it was arson.

At their final meeting with the Minister of Internal Affairs, Ron offered Global Care's help, medically and educationally, to the Albanian government. In addition, they would send out two nurses to teach paediatric care. There was a sad and a happy outcome to that meeting. When a lorryload of aid arrived at the hospital, it was promptly surrounded by about 1,000 Albanians who saw no reason for the "foolish" children to be given clothing and toys that their own children had never had. So rather violently they began to help themselves and stripped the aid lorry bare. The alarmed aid workers took the two nurses back to England with them for their own safety.

Janet never forgot the badly disfigured young girl, whom she called Lucy. Ron had taken a photograph of her, which was helpful when enlisting the aid of a kind British plastic surgeon. A few months later, Janet went down to Heathrow to meet a small party off the plane. Ron was escorting two girls along the tarmac, while interpreter Evis was pushing a wheelchair holding a little figure in a navy blue anorak and with a white cap pulled well down to hide her shorn head and some of her burns.

The little girl, from one of the poorest Albanian institutions, was admitted for surgery at a modern private hospital in Birmingham, England. However, Lucy didn't come on her own; she brought Albanian head lice to the top hospital. Lucy had a number of operations, which helped to improve her looks, and both she and Evis returned home to Albania a few months later. "They climbed into the back seat of my car – and into my life," said Janet, who has continued to support Lucy and keeps in touch with her through Evis and her mother Monda.

Chapter 14

A LETTER FROM ALBANIA - AT LAST

The government official who met Sali wasn't the only person who had been listening to Luan Mateu's programmes. At last, Sali Rahmani and all at Trans World Radio and ECM had the letter they had been waiting for. Early in 1991, the first listener's letter from Albania arrived, twenty-three years after ECM had first started broadcasting into the country, and eighteen years since Sali had begun his programmes. "I was so excited, extremely surprised, but very happy when I received the letter," said Sali. "I didn't open it for an hour as I was so busy phoning my friends to tell them. But I knew this was the beginning of something beautiful."

The letter was from Veria, an Albanian widower in Fier. He told Sali he had been secretly listening to his programme for a long time in the cellar of his home with his ten-year-old daughter. Veria, who was from an Orthodox background, had made a small altar out of a table, on top of which he had placed the radio and some bread and wine so the two of them could share communion as instructed by the programme. He wrote, "I was scared my daughter might tell her friends about the programme, but government officials never found out. I was not scared of going to jail, but I was afraid of losing my close friend, the radio."

Sali wrote back and invited him to a Christian camp that he, Stephen Bell, and others had been running since 1988 for Kosovar Albanians in Leptokaria, about 100 kilometres south-west of Thessalonica in Greece – never really believing he would attend. In July 1991, Sali was giving a talk at the camp when his wife Helen told him an Albanian, Veria, had arrived looking for Luan Mateu.

Sali was speechless. He apologized to the twenty campers and said he had to have a break as this was a very important day. He rushed over to Veria and they embraced each other. Veria said he had travelled the 300 kilometres in a lorry, crossing the Albanian border into Greece. He had made his way to Leptokaria and kept asking the locals until he found someone who could tell him where the camp was. Veria spent the week there, returning the same way to Fier as he had come. He later became one of the founding members of the church in Fier.

After Veria's letter, many started to arrive from Albania on a regular basis, including some from Berti. However, even Sali was surprised when in early 1992 he received a neatly written letter from a nine-year-old girl from Lushnjë.

Esmeralda Shahini was playing outside her house in Lushnjë when she noticed a leaflet on the pavement, which said, "If you are interested in God and Jesus' good news and would like a Bible, write to us." There then followed a box number and the frequency for Trans World Radio's *Way of Peace* programme. Esmeralda was intrigued, so she wrote a letter and then surprised her mum by asking her for the money for a stamp. Her mother was even more amazed when she learned the subject of the letter. Nevertheless, because she had been brought up an Orthodox and wanted her daughter to continue in the faith, she paid for the stamp. Although it had been illegal to listen to a foreign radio station, and particularly one talking about religion, Esmeralda persuaded her fifteen-year-old sister Senola and their parents Llambi and Parashqevi to join her in listening to the Trans World Radio programme. They enjoyed it so much that they continued listening. Later Esmeralda said she had a vivid dream one night that there was a fire in her house, and next morning her Bible arrived from ECM via Trans World Radio. Eagerly she opened it and began reading. "I read the Bible all the time and really enjoyed it."

Her parents had been brought up as Orthodox, but they hadn't gone to church for thirty-five years as Enver Hoxha had forbidden it. The leader had been so impressed with China's Chairman Mao and his Cultural Revolution, launched in August 1966, that he decided to copy him. Intellectuals were sent into the countryside to work in the factories and farms with the ordinary people. Women were encouraged to join the labour force and religion was blamed for oppressing and exploiting the people in the past.

In 1967 Hoxha said, "Islam has been the ideology of the Turkish occupier. The Orthodox religion has been the ideology of the Greek chauvinists who have occupied the country in the past, and Catholicism – with the Vatican at its centre – has been the ideology of the Italian invaders, Austrian imperialism, and Italian fascism."

Years later Berti remembered himself as a ten-year-old watching a mob of about 200 or 300 people demolishing the big Catholic Church in Laç in 1967. Berti said the local Party secretary led the group of mostly young people to the church, armed with sledgehammers. As the mob got to work, the secretary whipped up the emotion, urging them to be more patriotic and more zealous than the crowds in other towns. Berti said that some of them later admitted they were scared, but felt they had to join the crowd. Some suspected there was money behind the icons, while others said believers had seen these holy relics shedding tears. Many refused to touch the icons, thinking it would bring them bad luck. However, Berti thought many icons had been moved to safety a few nights previously.

Although Enver Hoxha could close religious buildings, he couldn't stop people believing and keeping to their traditions. There were many stories of brave priests who hid their vestments but continued to carry out their priestly duties and baptized babies. Worshippers also continued to observe Christmas and Easter in secret, since Hoxha had outlawed these festivals. He wanted the people to concentrate on New Year, when a factory or farm would announce the last year's achievements and their aims for the coming year. At New Year, everyone was encouraged to have a family meal at home, and the government would help the people by doubling their meat ration just for that week. At the meal, people were expected to drink three toasts with raki, beer, or wine. The first toast was to long life for Enver Hoxha and the party, the second was to thank everyone that you had had a good life in freedom and with food, and the third one was to wish everyone a happy New Year. However, many people, like letter writer Esmeralda's parents Llambi and Parashqevi, chose to celebrate still in the traditional way, even if they couldn't go to church. Like many Orthodox families, they would eat hard-boiled eggs at Easter in secret, and paint the shells red to remind them of Christ's blood and death on the cross, and would enjoy a family meal at Christmas and at Easter.

Llambi, who was a chemist in a food factory, and Parashqevi, an economist who worked in a plastics factory, said that to hide the evidence they would flush the shells down the toilet, while they knew of other families who would bury them in the garden. Even then, Parashqevi said, people had to be careful on feast days. Sometimes Communist officials would arrive unexpectedly on Christmas Day or Easter Day, saying they were checking whether the house was tidy or the bathroom was clean. In reality, it was to see what they were eating, who was there, and whether they had bought in special food for a celebratory feast. Even more deviously, colleagues from work would be sent to call unexpectedly and report on what they had seen.

Esmeralda and her sister Senola continued to listen regularly with their family to the Trans World Radio programme. By 1992, the political situation had eased and it wasn't so dangerous to be seen having an interest in religion. Quite often Esmeralda would invite some of her friends to come round to her house and listen as well. "I was a little scared," recalled Esmeralda, "but I wanted to know more and more about the Bible." She wrote another three times to the radio station and has kept all her replies, plus the Bible and literature they sent.

The family were delighted one day to receive a telegram from Luan Mateu inviting them to come along that summer to Vlorë for the first ever summer camp they were holding in Albania for listeners of the radio programme. The whole family went along, and Esmeralda said, "It was a very special camp. I enjoyed hearing the Bible stories and playing on the beach." At the end of the week, Esmeralda told Sali, "This is like heaven. Can we do the same things when we go home? I have already asked my parents and they have said yes."

Another early letter writer to ECM via Trans World Radio was

Berti. As well as providing a good business, one of the other advantages of the kiosk was that it was a safe postal address for his correspondence to ECM through Trans World Radio. "What are you interested in?" they wrote back after one of his letters in 1990. "I want to know more about God," said Berti. "The answers are in the Bible," they said. "What is the Bible?" replied Berti, who then asked if they would send him one, which they did. Trans World Radio and ECM also recommended a correspondence course to him, which he persuaded another friend, Kashmiri, a Kosovan engineer at a food factory, to translate.

One day Berti was delighted to receive a letter from England, from a Christian who had marked his Soon Bible Correspondence Course work, a reply he still has today. It was from Dr Leonard Loose, of Brancaster Staithe, King's Lynn. The son of a Norfolk fisherman, Dr Loose was awarded a first-class honours and then a PhD in botany before going out to India as a missionary in 1939 to the Mar Thoma School in Kerala. He, his wife, and their four sons returned to England in 1948, where he taught at Fakenham Grammar School until he retired. During his retirement, he helped to mark the Soon correspondence course and gave Berti 194 marks out of 200 and 195 out of 200 for his two papers. He wrote: "Dear Albert, this is the first Bible study paper that has come to me from Albania. I thank the living God and Saviour Jesus Christ that you had this opportunity to send this letter to me. Your handwriting is excellent, your use of the English language is very good, and your answers show you have a clear understanding of what you have read from the Bible."

One day Kashmiri warned Berti, "You had better be careful: people are watching you."

"I hope they are," replied a confident Berti, "I hope they find God."

By now, he was desperate to find out everything he could about God, and when he saw an advertisement in a local paper for another correspondence course, in Italian, through a Catholic church in Lezha, he applied – even though he couldn't speak Italian. As well as taking a chance by writing to the radio station, Berti took an even bigger risk by confiding in a friend, Kristaq, who was an army officer in the Rapid Defence Force, asking him to translate the Italian replies into Albanian. They took about three or four weeks to arrive and were brought faithfully to the kiosk by a postwoman, Sadate. "For the next two years I wasn't a believer with all my heart," admitted Berti. "But I wanted to learn, I wanted to do well on the correspondence courses and to get top marks."

In 1992 the government announced the first of its six-monthly military reforms, and Berti volunteered to leave the army. Despite him being highly experienced and highly qualified, they agreed to let him go. In July 1992 Berti marched out of the safe world of the military with its guaranteed salary, into the more precarious world of self-employment. He continued to run the kiosk with Ladi, while listening to Trans World Radio, and kept on with the correspondence courses, as well as looking after his wife and bringing up their young family.

In the spring of 1993, Berti was surprised to receive a telegram inviting him to join a number of Albanians at a camp that June in Vlorë, about a couple of hours' drive south of Lushnjë. It was from ECM via Trans World Radio and signed Luan Mateu.

Chapter 15

GOD HAS BEEN STOLEN FROM US FOR FORTY-SEVEN YEARS

In the time since Enver Hoxha had died, Christians had been amazed by all that had happened in Albania. But even they were staggered when, in July 1991, the government of a country which just over twenty-four years previously had "abolished God" invited Christians to come and show them "how to live properly". Many Christians had been praying and preparing for this day for years, but they hadn't expected their prayers to be answered in this way.

The Christians asked the government where they could hold a rally, and were given the keys to the Qemal Strafa, the main football stadium in the capital Tirana, where England had played two years earlier. It was the equivalent of the British government giving Christians control of Wembley Stadium. At the opening event, the Albanian Minister of Culture, Arta Dade, told the crowds, "Our country needs spiritual things." A total of 120 Christians came, including Brother Andrew. Stephen Bell and eight others travelled together by minibus from Prishtina. They were worried about what would happen if border officials discovered their Christian songsheets or New Testaments; even worse, these were in Albanian, a language despised by the

Yugoslavs. However, as they crossed the Yugoslavian/Albanian border at Hani Hoti, north of Shkodra, they couldn't have had two more different receptions.

At the Yugoslavian side of the border they mumbled vague answers to officials who wondered why they wanted to go to a crazy place like Albania, carefully avoiding any mention of Christianity. As soon as they drove the 100 metres to the Albanian side, they were welcomed like long-lost friends. As the team all spoke fluent Albanian, the armed border guards and customs officials insisted they bring out their guitars and sing some Christian songs – all within earshot of the Yugoslav guards on the other side of the border. Stephen recalled, "It was mind-blowing. In Kosovo and Yugoslavia we were very cautious, but in Albania we were placed on a pedestal as border guards begged us, 'Be our missionaries.'"

Sali Rahmani had also been invited to Tirana, and he decided to drive with his family from ECM in Vienna to Albania, and then on to Greece, where he was again leading the summer camp. On leaving Austria, the first border they came to was Slovenia. What he didn't know was that he wasn't the only person visiting that country on 27 June 1991. The Yugoslav army arrived to invade Slovenia, because as part of the break-up of Yugoslavia the Slovene parliament had declared its independence two days earlier after a national referendum. "When we arrived at the border," recalled Sali, "there were soldiers and cars everywhere." Border guards told them they couldn't go any farther because of the military situation.

"But I have got to get to Albania for a conference," replied Sali, who persisted in trying to cross the border, despite his wife Helen begging him to stop and turn round.

The guards said troops and tanks were coming and it was

too dangerous. In the end, the officials decided to let the family through into Slovenia to see the situation for themselves. Sali was less than ten minutes in Slovenia. He saw the Yugoslav tanks and soldiers coming towards him and decided it was time for a swift exit. With a rapid U-turn the Rahmani family headed for the safety of Austria, just making it there before the Yugoslav Air Force bombed the border post. "I was heartbroken," said Sali. "After all those years of broadcasting to Albania and now the first big public Christian meeting for fifty years, and I couldn't be there."

Incidentally, the Slovenian Territorial Defence Forces and the police kept the Yugoslav army at bay. On 7 July, the Yugoslavs agreed to a ceasefire brokered by the European Union.

Many Albanians were delighted to meet the Christians and called the campaign *Zoti e do Shqipërinë*, which is translated "God loves Albania." They put up six-metre by three-metre banners and notices all round the capital advertising the event, including in the main square, where Enver Hoxha's statue had been until the crowds pulled it down. Stephen Bell volunteered to help with one of the thirteen open-air preaching groups. "It was amazing: it was like going back to biblical times," he said. "There were crowds of people. I had four mornings to preach through John's Gospel in which I had one hour to prepare and then two hours to preach. There were thirteen groups, each with a different person preaching from John's Gospel. I had about fifty people in my group, but it was just a sea of faces. I preached until I got a tap on the shoulder to say it was lunch and time to close the meeting."

The visiting Christians were prepared, bringing with them 50,000 New Testaments, 25,000 John's Gospels and copies of

Floyd McClung's book *The Father Heart of God*, all of which they distributed. Stephen said, "We watched thousands clamour for the Word of God. They were 'cannibalizing' whole boxes of New Testaments like piranhas as we took them to the crowds, and many became Christians during those meetings." He added, "Once I was asked to take one big box containing a few hundred New Testaments around the stadium from one exit to another one. I had safely negotiated half the stadium perimeter when someone realized I had Bibles. Suddenly a horde of Albanians jumped all over me, grabbing desperately into the box!"

Stephen said he had been warned that they should distribute the Bibles strategically during the two-week campaign, otherwise they would all disappear in a flash and those needing them most would have to go without. "So I bent right over the box to protect the Bibles, while the crowd of fifty grabbed," said Stephen. "It became dark as the sun was obliterated by the assailing crowd. I started to fear for my own safety until suddenly I began to feel an easing of pressure and was aware of sunlight. Huge Hank, a six-foot-six-inch Dutchman, who was in charge of the team logistics, had come. Like a friendly giant he was taking the hands off me one by one. I picked myself up and we continued the mission."

Stephen Etches, of ECM, translated the New Testament and then the whole of the Bible into modern Albanian, a language different to any other European language. Stephen finished translating the complete Bible in the early 1990s, having gone back to the original Greek and Hebrew to get an accurate translation. A leather-bound copy of the first translation was sent to the President of Albania, Sali Berisha. "Stephen was a brilliant linguist and it was a privilege to help him with this task," said Sali. "I just wish I had been there to see the joy of the Albanians as they were given the New Testaments in their own language."

Incidentally, work on the first Albanian New Testament began in 1819 and it was printed on Corfu in 1827. It was later revised and was reprinted in Athens in 1858.[1]

After a hectic two weeks with the Tirana mission Stephen Bell returned to Prishtina, leaving his eight friends at Struga on the Albanian/Macedonian border. He caught a bus to Skopje, Mother Teresa's birthplace, and the place where Sali Rahmani was healed. During the three-and-a-half hour ride he started talking to the young student next to him, who was studying economics at university. They exchanged addresses and Stephen later visited him; a few weeks later he heard that he had become a Christian and was getting baptized.

Although the Christian campaign had been big news in Tirana, with 8,000 Albanians at the stadium, the rest of the country had no idea what was happening, as it did not make the news or national TV. For Berti and the others away from the capital it would be another two years before churches were established in their towns.

Once the euphoria and initial enthusiasm of a big Christian rally was over, the problem was how to start a church in Albania, a country the size of Wales, where in the words of one Albanian, "God has been stolen from us for forty-seven years."

In October 1991, Christians decided one of the ways to help the church was to form an umbrella organization, which they called the Albanian Encouragement Project. The purpose of this was first, to enable organizations and churches to cooperate while remaining autonomous in their individual ministries, second, to present a united front to the Albanian government and international organizations, and third, to exchange information and communicate with each other to avoid duplication of work. However, the main aim was to help and encourage the Albanian Christians, to plant churches, and to help them grow.

The first chairman of the group was Jack Murray, who was also the ECM International director. Born in Maypole, Ayrshire, in 1928, Jack left school at fourteen to train as an electrician. He became a Christian as a teenager under the ministry of Dr Peter Connelly and went to Bible college before joining ECM, working in Italy and then Albania. He spent one week in every three months for three years in Tirana developing the project. "The office was one empty room and I remember taking out funds from Britain to buy the first office equipment," he recalled.

After a holiday in England and a meeting with ECM, Stephen Bell decided he had to return to Albania to live there and help the new church. On 1 October 1991 he left Prishtina University, having successfully completed his course, and set off to Albania for the third time. This time he arrived in Sarande by ferry from Corfu, and was surprised to be greeted by four soldiers, who all recognized him from the rally and were carrying New Testaments given out in Tirana. "As we entered Albania I was suddenly struck by fear," he recalled. "Where on earth would I find food to eat? All around me was abject poverty and dilapidation. However, as I journeyed on the rickety Chinese bus through the countryside and mountains, I was really encouraged by a thought from God. 'See these people, Stephen, my people. They are all alive, aren't they? Wherever you see one of my Albanians, there is surely bread for you within four hours' walk. You'll be OK.'"

And he was. The obvious place to go was Tirana, where the rally had been held. As he made his way to the capital, wondering where he should live, a stranger ran up to him shouting, "Stephen, maybe you don't know me, but I became a Christian in your Bible study group in the park in July." The nineteen-year-old student, Klodian, invited him to share his room in his family's home, and his parents, Ismet and Violeta, adopted Stephen as a "son". Later, Ismet escorted Stephen on his church trips, as it was not easy for a foreigner to travel round Albania on his own in those days.

One day Stephen was asked to drive a borrowed car seventy kilometres to Elbasan, the industrial town where Berti Dosti had worked as a young man, to show the *Jesus* film at a believer's house. He arrived at Anastas's home, and that's when the problems started. The person who was supposed to bring the film from Greece hadn't arrived. Then Stephen became violently sick, and as a result of his constant retching and toilet visits he neglected to guard the car. As night fell at 5 p.m. the unguarded car was robbed – of its windscreen!

The next day Stephen had no option but to drive back over the mountains in the freezing December weather in a car minus its windscreen, thinking he would have to buy a replacement back in Tirana. He never dreamt he would see the windscreen again, but two days later Stephen had his most unusual Christmas present. On Christmas Day 1991, Anastas, plus the car owner and a stranger, arrived at his house, having driven the seventy kilometres from Elbasan to Tirana to see him. Anastas had tracked down the thief and challenged him about the windscreen, which he said belonged to "God's messenger", and warned him about the consequences of his wrongdoing. "Such was the thief's conviction," said Stephen, "that not only did he apologize, but he brought the windscreen to me in person, asked for my forgiveness, and said he wanted to become a Christian. I forgave him, hugged him, and shared one of my Christmas presents from my parents in England with him, a Mars bar – an unknown delight in those early days in Albania."

At the end of 1991 and in early 1992 hundreds of missionaries flocked into the country to help set up new churches. A surge of people became Christians over the next twelve to eighteen months as the church spread out from Tirana into the rest of the country. At the time Stephen said, "Albanian believers are youngish, eighteen to forty years old, and really keen to learn. It was exciting to be with them, and they are really excited too about what God is doing in their once closed homeland."

But Stephen needed some help with his church work. This was particularly obvious at the end of the first week of the Vlorë August camp in the summer of 1992, when Stephen left to go to Germany to become engaged to Tabita. The romance had started when Stephen had gone with Sali Rahmani to Stuttgart in Germany to visit Albanian refugees there. One evening they were invited to bring twenty Albanians to a barbecue at the home of a Christian family, the Sijantas, who had a daughter, Tabita. Three years later, they returned to Stuttgart and this time used the Sijantas' house as a mission base. Later, when they held a third Christian campaign, this time in Freiburg in Bavaria, they invited Tabita to join the team. Tabita had noticed Stephen, but he wasn't aware of anything until he found out that Tabita had checked with friends whether he was married or not. They started going out, and eventually Stephen proposed to her, on condition that she should first see what life was like in Albania, so she knew what she was letting herself in for. Tabita, who had been brought up in Germany, was shocked by the poverty in Albania. She wrote home to her family, "Life here is a little different: we must wait two hours for paraffin, water doesn't come all day, electricity occasionally gets cut off, and one must search the 'shops' for food." Despite all this Tabita said yes to marriage and yes to Albania, and the couple began preparing for their wedding on Saturday 13 April 1993, in Germany.

When Stephen returned to Albania, an excited Sali Rahmani met him and told him that while he was away during the second week of the camps, three Albanians had been converted and baptized. What's more, Gëzim, Lida, and Xhovi wanted to continue the camp meetings by starting churches in their home towns of Berat and Fier, and they asked Stephen to lead them. He agreed, even though the towns were up to 100 miles away from his home in Tirana.

Two girls around twenty years old began to attend the fellowship at Fier. They came by bus from the town of Patos. Because it was dark after the Fier meeting, some of the believers, including Stephen, arranged to drive them the eleven kilometres back home. Alma, the elder of the two, who had been a listener of Sali's radio programmes, regularly invited her friends to come along. In the end, she asked if Stephen could hold meetings at her parents' house in Patos as she had fifteen friends who wanted to come. "Of course I said yes, while hastily consulting my diary for more of that precious commodity called time," recalled Stephen. Twenty-six friends came to that first meeting, twenty-five of whom were women, plus a twelve-year-old boy, Bledi, and Stephen, who led the church until 1997, when Murray Cotter took over.

Then in December, Stephen and Sali led three evangelistic rallies in Tirana, with all of the guests invited by telegram. There were 270 at the first meeting, 170 a week later, and seventy at the third meeting, with Stephen the only Christian among them! At Christmas 1992 he wrote home to say, "These last four months must be among the most fulfilling and yet demanding of my life." He had set himself a punishing schedule of going every Saturday to Berat, seventy-five miles away, to take an adult meeting, and then a children's meeting the following morning, before going on another thirty miles for a similar meeting in Fier. On Mondays, he led an adults' meeting in Fier, going back on Tuesdays to take a Bible study in Berat and returning on the Wednesday to take a Bible study in Tirana. Thursday and Friday were spent at home. For the first few months, he had to travel by public transport, but was later able to obtain a front-wheel-drive vehicle, which made the tortuous travelling over poorly maintained roads a little easier.

As these two churches developed into four in the autumn of 1992, the issue arose of who would take care of them while Stephen was on home leave from April to November 1993 to get married.

He decided the ideal person was his friend Gani in Prishtina. Gani had been on a three-month Bible course and was excellent at encouraging new Albanian Christians to grow in the faith, as well as answering radio listeners' letters, translating documents, and helping new missionaries adjust to the country. However, to do that he would have to persuade Gani to give up a good university job and to get his family to leave Kosovo and to come back to what Gani called "his promised land of Albania". In November 1992 he invited Gani and Adile to meet him in Vlorë. To Stephen's surprise, Adile was the more receptive to his plans. "I feel we should say yes," she told her husband, "and we should start in three or four weeks' time." Gani was shocked, but agreed, and they went home to break the news to their three children.

Understandably, they were not too keen on the idea, nor

was Gani's horrified mother, who said to Adile, "Tell him not to go, and don't take the children." But on 15 January 1993, the family, who were now supported by ECM, left Prishtina by truck and by bus, and for political reasons drove to their new home in Tirana via Macedonia, because going through Montenegro was too dangerous.

As it turned out, 1993 was a difficult year and a tough baptism for the Smolica family. Gani said, "I was a spiritual sheep and a shepherd at the same time. I had had hardly any training, so I was learning from Stephen and then teaching others." Adile said, "It was difficult bringing up the children there." After the relatively good lifestyle in Kosovo, she found life in Albania much harder. "I couldn't find any meat to buy, and nowhere was very clean," she admitted.

Just as they were settling down to life in Tirana, Stephen left them on Sunday 14 March to go home to England and Germany for his wedding. He handed over full responsibility for the Fier, Berat, Tirana, and Patos churches to Gani.

In Germany, everyone gets married formally at a registry office, and then those who want to can get married in church afterwards. Stephen and Tabita had the civil ceremony in Stuttgart on Tuesday 30 March, followed by a church service on Tuesday 3 April. The couple enjoyed the church wedding, but Stephen wasn't impressed by the town hall ceremony, which he considered was "pagan". "Even before the ceremony started," recalled Stephen, "I think the well-meaning German mayor interpreted my body language as being insolent and not interested in the proceedings." After the civil ceremony, Stephen and Tabita went shopping for the first time as Mr and Mrs Bell. However, when they returned to Tabita's parents at lunchtime that day, her dad said they had to go to the Town Hall and to speak to the mayor urgently.

As Stephen couldn't speak German, Tabita had to translate. The mayor said he had checked out Stephen on his computer and accused him of being a bigamist, warning him that he could go to jail. It transpired that five years earlier, the mayor had conducted a ceremony for a soldier called Stephen Bell, and he thought Tabita's husband was the same person. "He took some convincing that I was a different person," added Stephen, who can now laugh at the incident.

"Missionary guilty of bigamy" – now that's a headline the author of this book never came across in his working life as a journalist. It's a story the tabloid papers would have paid me good money for.

The couple started married life in November 1993 in Fier, where Stephen had found a flat for them. It had one bedroom, a living room/kitchen, a two-metre by two-and-a-half-metre study, and a bathroom with even hot water and a Western toilet, rather than the usual Eastern hole in the floor. Another bonus was that in return for a small salary, a neighbour armed with a rifle agreed to look after their car twenty-four hours a day so it wouldn't be stolen.

Chapter 16

FACE TO FACE WITH AN ANGRY MOB IN LAÇ

The summer camp in Vlorë in June 1993 hadn't got off to a good start. As Berti arrived at the site, which was used as an orphanage during term time, he was met with blank looks as he announced, "I've come to see Luan Mateu." Then someone remembered it was the name Sali Rahmani's used for his Trans World Radio broadcasts. The camp had been set up to help churches in the rest of Albania, away from the capital Tirana. Sali, Stephen, and Gani had gone through all the letters they had received from Albanian listeners and invited those from Fier, Berat, and Lushnjë to come along to a two-week summer camp to meet each other, and to receive some Christian teaching. The trouble was that no one knew how many would turn up. Therefore, when the Albanians received a telegram inviting them to a free holiday, with good food at a nice location, they decided to bring their whole family along.

It was total chaos. By the time Berti, who had left his children with his wife Tatjana in Lushnjë, arrived, all the beds in the dormitory had gone. Berti, used to military discipline and to everything being done in an organized fashion, was not impressed. It was difficult to find a place to sleep, and when he couldn't find any food to eat he said to himself, "That's it. Things are so bad I'm going home in the morning." Having found a small space to put down his bed and not having had the best night's sleep, he got up early and walked down the stairs with his bags. One of the helpers saw him and rushed to find Gani, who dashed across, just catching Berti as he left the site.

"Why are you leaving?" said Gani, who was meeting Berti for the first time.

"I don't like anything here, and besides it doesn't seem like a camp," he replied.

Gani knew that if one person left on the second day, others would follow, and the whole campaign to reach Christians in the south of the country would fail disastrously at the first attempt. Thinking on his feet, Gani said, "Stay for my sake: I will arrange things for you." Gani was as good as his word. He found a bunk bed with the foreign team of camp workers, sorted out the food problem, and introduced Berti to Sali. "It wasn't a very emotional meeting," recalled Sali. "Although I was very excited to meet him, I could see that he was a military man, who was very serious and intelligent, so I welcomed him and just stayed talking to him for a few minutes."

Berti was impressed and felt so privileged that he had to stay. As he admitted later, it was a turning point in his life. He soon adjusted to camp life, enjoying the daily routine of breakfast, then worship and Bible study before going to the beach. After lunch, there was time to relax, before another Bible study and an evening service.

Sali said later that he couldn't fail to be impressed by Berti, a model student who took studying so seriously and who asked many profound questions, as he had done in his letters to the radio station. He had also brought along the certificates from all his various correspondence courses. At the Bible study, the first to arrive was always Berti. He was immaculately dressed, not a hair out of place, and sitting at his desk with his pencils lined up, as though on a military parade, eagerly waiting for the lecturer to begin. He also had his Bible and notebook ready and was quick to answer the questions or take notes.

Berti said that in all those years of listening to the radio he had heard about worship, taking the Lord's Supper at communion, and praying to God. "But suddenly, at the camp, things I had heard about on the radio were happening all around me, and I began to understand. I was with other Christians and I started to think differently," he recalled. By the end of the third day, Berti had forgotten all about the bad start to camp and was now enjoying everything.

However, on the fourth day he had a rude awakening at 5:30 a.m. His kiosk partner Ladi was outside, sounding his car's horn. When Berti went out to see him, he said, "You've got to come: your brother's had an accident." He didn't know any more details, but he went to see Sali and said for the second time in four days that he was leaving camp. This time Sali knew it was more serious, and he said a quick prayer with Berti. Before Berti dashed off, they asked him if they could visit him at his house, as they knew he wouldn't come back to the camp. "Yes, you are very welcome," said Berti, before rushing off for the seven-and-a-half-hour journey to Laç, stopping off in Lushnjë just long enough to pick up Tatjana. She had been all set to go to Korçë to visit her family.

Tatjana had the TV on, but wasn't watching it when the announcement came that a police officer had been injured in Laç. They interviewed Iliri in the hospital about what happened, and it was only then that Tatjana recognized the voice and turned round to see her brother-in-law on TV. Iliri, who had retired from the army two years before and joined the police, was walking in Laç when he saw two people pushing a woman into a car. Although not on duty, he was in uniform, and tried to stop the car. When he leaned in to grab the car keys, one of the men stabbed Iliri twice, once in the ribs and once in the lung. Iliri fainted in the road, while the other three, two brothers and a sister, drove off. Iliri was taken in a helicopter to the hospital at Lezha.

By this time, a rumour had spread around the town that the police had beaten up two people. The crowd called a general strike and surrounded the police station. "When we arrived," said Berti, "the roads were full of people with rocks and stones. There must have been a few thousand people on the streets. We were very afraid, but we still didn't know then all that had happened. People were very aggressive and they were putting up barriers to blockade roads." If they had known Berti was Iliri's brother they would have attacked him as well. Some knew Iliri had a brother in Lushnjë, but fortunately, no one realized Berti was driving through a hostile crowd in a Lushnjë car with an LU number plate.

When Berti and Tatjana made their way to Iliri's house, neighbours told them what had happened. They urged the Dostis to leave at once and not let anyone know who they were or why they had come. They were told Iliri had been taken to the hospital in Lezha, where Iliri's wife's family lived. Again, Ladi drove the road between Laç and Lezha, a journey that Berti had done as a young child in a lorry when his father had moved military base. This journey was more nerve-racking, and Berti was more nervous than the last time. Frustratingly, when they got to Lezha Hospital they found Iliri had been taken to Tirana from

Laç, which meant a drive of almost another hour.

After a week in hospital, Iliri's lung recovered and he was able to go home. Berti also returned home, but by then it was too late to go back to camp. However, the Christian leaders were so impressed in the short time they had seen Berti that that they decided to let him run the camp the following year.

As for the crowd in Laç, the police called for the Rapid Response Force, who cleared the streets. The bad feeling between the police and the local people lasted for months.

Iliri was reprimanded for interfering when he wasn't on duty. He was demoted to sergeant, not allowed to go back to work in Laç and sent to Lezhna, where he became very bitter with the way he had been treated. After two more years in the police force, he retired in 2005.

Chapter 17

A TEARFUL REUNION

Berti had never thought about his mother that much – until a strange dream in July 1992. As he had not seen Antoneta since he was three years old, he had very few memories of her. He could hardly remember what she looked like, particularly as he didn't have any pictures of her, and had not seen her, or even tried to see her, for the last thirty-two years.

Berti doesn't know why his mother suddenly came into his mind. Whether it was because he was questioning everything in his search for faith, he is not sure. But he does know that it was a vivid dream. "She was dressed in black," recalled Berti. "She was wailing, and I saw her face to face across a room. She said to me, 'Why don't you meet me, why haven't you tried to find me?'" When Berti woke up, he tried to convince himself he didn't believe in dreams. Besides, he had been brought up in Communist Albania, where anything supernatural or paranormal was laughed at. The authorities said God didn't exist, so obviously He wouldn't speak through dreams. They said no one should believe in superstitions, particularly in the twentieth century, and certainly not someone trained as an officer in the Albanian army. But the dream wouldn't go away. What if he did try to find his mother, he wondered one day. The more he thought about it, the more he realized how difficult it would be. Where could he start? He didn't dare ask his father, because he had forbidden Berti to have any contact with his mother. He didn't know where she lived, and didn't have any recent photographs of her. In addition, his mother could have remarried and changed her name, or she might not even be alive. Besides, if he did try to contact his mother he would be going against his father's will, something which was unacceptable in Albanian family life. His father had warned him, "If you meet your mother, you can forget me. I won't talk to you ever again."

Berti knew he couldn't go to any relatives for help, as they would immediately tell his father. Moreover, he couldn't go to his older brother Iliri: he had been told by the family that she was a bad mother, and he had believed them. But despite all the problems and barriers, Berti decided he ought to make one attempt to find her. If he didn't, he might regret it for the rest of his life.

Berti booked a fortnight's leave and headed with Tatjana to Korçë, the only place where he knew his mother had lived, and so the obvious place to start the search. It was strange coming back to the place of his birth. He hadn't returned there for more than thirty years, apart from a brief visit to the market with his stepmother's father when he thought he might have seen his mother in a crowd. Despite it being a long time since he had been in Korçë, he did manage to find the neighbourhood where they used to live, with a general store on a street corner. He went in and saw a woman who must have been about his mother's age behind the counter, so asked her, "Excuse me, do you know Antoneta Dosti?"

The shop woman went pale, was silent for a long time, and then, without looking at Berti, said, "No, I don't know that woman." Berti thought it was very strange, but thanked her and left. What he didn't know until much later was that the shopkeeper was a good friend of Antoneta's, but she had been too frightened to say anything.

He had a vague memory that his mother had worked as a waitress, so he went to the town's biggest bar, the Agimi. He spoke to one of the staff, who to his amazement said Antoneta had worked there, but didn't now. She thought that she still lived in the house where Berti had lived as a baby, and gave him the address. Fortunately for Berti the neighbourhood hadn't changed that much, as the houses were older and had the equivalent of preservation orders on them, so he soon recognized his old home. But what should he do next? He observed the house for some time and saw a man and then a younger man leave, but he still wasn't sure about going up to the door.

He decided to persuade some children to knock on the door to check that his mother was alone. When she answered, Berti recognized his mother, and a few minutes later he went and knocked on the door himself. As soon as she answered, she recognized him and invited him in. She didn't want to show any emotion in public, but as soon as he was inside she hugged him and cried.

"Why didn't you come before? I have waited so long," she sobbed. They hugged for some time and then she fainted. Berti didn't know what to do, so placed her on the settee. Fortunately a glass of water soon revived her. They then told each other what had happened to them in the intervening years. Berti talked about his upbringing and his time at school and in the army before mentioning his marriage and their two children, daughter Alta and son Dorian. He said he had lived with his stepmother, who worked as a polisher in a carpentry business, from the age of six to fourteen, when he went away to school.

Antoneta explained that she had tried to contact him, and had sent him clothes and sweets on his birthday for many years, but the parcels had always been returned unopened. She knew he had moved to Lushnjë and had asked people she knew, "Can you find anything out about my Berti?" But they never came back with any news. She spoke to her relatives, but they were scared of Berti's father, who said, "Don't tell her anything." Antoneta said she had remarried, had later had a son, and now had two grandchildren. She said when she first met her second husband he had promised that he would allow her to meet Berti again after they got married. But Antoneta said he became very jealous and possessive, later forbidding her to try to track down her son. She admitted it had not been a happy marriage.

After an emotional hour of swapping news, Berti thought he had better return to Tatjana, who had been waiting patiently for him. As he left, his mother made him promise that he would come back and see her again.

Over the next twelve months they managed to meet secretly, either at the hotel or in the houses of friends.

However, his father eventually found out and told his other son, Iliri. The next time Berti met his father and brother it was a stormy meeting.

"Why have you betrayed me?" demanded his father. "We looked after you because of her."

Berti tried to explain to them both: "I haven't betrayed you, but I just wanted to meet my mother."

As the row continued, Berti told them, "I haven't lost my love for you. But no one can stop me meeting my mother." He added, "One day she will die, and I will ask myself, 'Why didn't I try to meet her?'"

Chapter 18

STARTING A CHURCH FROM SCRATCH

On Friday 23 July 1993, at 6:30 p.m., the church in Lushnjë was resurrected after a gap of nearly half a century.

Following the summer camp at Vlorë in 1993, the missionaries decided to set up a church in Lushnjë and asked Berti and others to gather as many friends as they could. The first meeting was held in Llambi's house, as their daughter, nine-year-old Esmeralda Shahini, had written to Trans World Radio and the family had enjoyed the camp so much. There were sixteen people at the service, including Llambi and his family, some of their neighbours, plus Berti and his friend Kashmiri, who had helped translate his correspondence course.

The first service was a very simple one and was led by Sali, Gani, and a Dutch missionary called Arnaud (whose name means "Albanian" in Turkish). It included singing and guitar playing, prayers, Bible reading, and a talk. During the service, the leaders asked the Albanians to say how they had heard about the radio programme, and then suggested they meet again in a week's time, when they would also start a children's meeting.

The next service was held in Berti's house, and within a month it was held there every week. Despite all that had happened with the radio broadcasts and the camps, it was no easy task starting a church in Lushnjë. Of all the Albanians who came to the first service, only Berti and his children turned up to the second one. Nevertheless, Gani and Arnaud, who came from Tirana, two hours' drive away every week, persevered. After the service, they slept at Berti's house before returning home the next morning. Even though she wasn't a Christian then, Tatjana said she didn't mind opening their house up and entertaining the visitors.

After the first meeting, they decided to ask Berti, because of his good organizational skills, to set up and lead the service. Berti taught the children while the missionaries took it in turn to preach. Gradually numbers increased, and as Berti and Tatjana's home became too small, they began to look for a room to rent for the church. In Lushnjë they found a dental clinic, where fifty people worked in twenty rooms. On the third floor was a large room used for meetings, which Berti's friend Dr Gjergji helped them to rent.

On Christmas Day 1993, at 11 a.m., the new Lushnjë church, now called the Way of Peace Church (in Albanian *Rruga e Paqes*) after the name of the Albanian programme on Trans World Radio, celebrated the first service there. A total of twenty-five people attended, already a healthy increase on the sixteen who had met at the first church meeting only five months before. The centre was ideal in every way bar one, which was the entrance. To get there, worshippers had to climb three sets of stairs, which were usually splattered with blood from the patients leaving after having had their dental treatment.

Party officials had used the room where the Christians met, in Enver Hoxha's time. Workers came there to study Hoxha's books, to discuss and underline passages, and then to memorize them, finishing by saying praise to Enver Hoxha. Now Christians were using the same room to study God's Word, to discuss and underline passages from the Bible, and to memorize verses, before finishing by saying and singing praises to God.

For the next few years, Berti continued to listen to the *Way of Peace* programme on the Trans World Radio station and to study their correspondence course, on top of working and looking after his family and the church. As well as running his kiosk, in March 1994 Berti also got a job as a waiter in a nearby café. But the owner wouldn't let him have a lunch break and go to a church Bible study. So the missionaries and local Christians came up with a novel solution. They would have a coffee at the café and talk about the Bible with Berti there.

He left the job in May that year to become an assistant to a lawyer, and although he couldn't type, he had an excellent tutor in Tatjana, who was doing a similar job in the town court. Berti soon moved on to a better job as a court official, which lasted only three months, as he was made redundant because of government cutbacks.

The next day, the wife of the lawyer to whom he had been an assistant called him. She had been so impressed with his work for her husband that she offered him a job typing legal documents. Although Berti didn't realize it then, it put him in a strategic position to help the victims of the pyramid selling scandal which would hit the country three years later.

By now, the ECM missionaries had set up six *Rruga e Paqes* or Way of Peace churches. They were: Tirana (overseen by Gani), Fier and Berat (Stephen Bell), Vlorë (Stephen led this church until Peter and Marie Hoffman moved there in May 1995), Patos (Stephen led this church until Murray Cotter took over in 1997), and Lushnjë (Gani led until November 1993, when Berti took over. He was the first Albanian to oversee a Way of Peace church).

Starting up churches was not easy, but an even more difficult task was to train the Albanian leaders, who had had no Christian teaching. Sali and Stephen decided the first step was to bring all the church leaders together in Berat on 17 November 1993. At their first meeting, they talked about training, growing as a Christian, and church life, and Stephen was so impressed by Berti that he offered to teach him how to preach. "It was a memorable conference," said Berti, "as I made a public stand about my faith to a large audience."

The following summer Tatjana and the children decided to go for the first time to the Vlorë camp, which Berti was leading. The camps were proving hugely popular: 120 people came in 1992, rising to more than 250 in the following two years. It was also a turning point for Tatjana. "I became a Christian there, and it changed my life," she said. "I feel such a different person now."

Every week for a few months Berti travelled to Fier, an hour's car journey away, for a teaching session at Stephen's house. In April 1994 Stephen decided Berti was ready to preach his first sermon. Until then Berti had led the services, but a missionary had always preached the sermon. Berti remembers he spoke on Colossians. First, he wrote the sermon down, sent it to Stephen, and then went to Fier to preach it to him, before he gave the talk to the Lushnjë congregation. "I was a little nervous preaching at first," said Berti, "but then I became more confident and really enjoyed it."

However, his teacher did not attend the Lushnjë service, as he and his pupil both agreed it would be too emotional an occasion. Stephen recalled, "I was very privileged, as I watched the Albanian church grow. I am one of God's workers, yet in a sense a mere bystander 'watching' the Albanian church as it grows. Although it is God who plants churches, we His servants must work our socks off in an attempt to keep pace with His initiatives."

Stephen, Gani, Sali and other missionaries certainly did work their socks off. Sali and Gani were travelling down from Tirana every week to Lushnjë, while Stephen came from Fier, where he had moved after he had married Tabita, and they all clocked up the miles to help the infant Albanian church.

Meanwhile, Tabita was also busy. In October 1995 she passed her final exam to qualify as psychologist, and the following year on 7 August she gave birth to their first daughter, Sheona Naemi. It wasn't an easy time for the proud parents, as baby Sheona suffered from pneumonia for the first two weeks of her life, but she then made a full recovery. With a third member of the Bell household, they decided their fourth-floor, one-bedroom flat was too small, so in October 1996 they moved into a bigger home in Fier, complete with a garden of lemon and orange trees and vines. The other big advantage was that they now had a wall and a yard where they could park their jeep without having to pay armed guards.

Stephen also realized that the Albanian church leaders needed more teaching, and two major initiatives were introduced in 1994. ECM decided that pastors and elders from the churches should form a denominational council which would oversee the churches and approve such matters as appointing new deacons, pastors, and elders. In addition, the board would try to maintain unity among the churches. Secondly, it was decided to set up a Bible school. The churches were growing fast, at 300 per cent per year. There were few Christians before Albania opened up, and therefore training the leaders and pastors was a priority. In a joint venture with three missions – Ancient World Outreach, the Greater European Mission, and ECM – they decided to start the Albanian Bible Institute (ABI). The first job was to find a coordinator, and they chose Barth Companjen, a Dutchman from Ancient World Outreach, who was an acknowledged Balkans expert. But who should be the director and dean of studies? The answer came very quickly. Frans Blok, who was Academic Dean of a Bible school in Holland, said, "We felt God calling us to the mission field, and to Albania specifically. We did not know much about the country, but decided to send a fax to the office of Barth Companjen in Greece." This was a guesthouse and office which served almost all the foreign missionaries in Albania in the first two chaotic years after the country opened up. "In this fax we told about our calling for Albania, our willingness to do what was needed, and our experience with the Bible school," he added. "Barth came back from Albania after a fourteen-hour trip by car, and the first thing he found in his office was our fax from Holland. You can imagine he was very surprised and excited about this apparently quick answer to his prayer."

Frans was appointed director and dean of studies, and he, his wife, and their three boys arrived in Albania in the summer of 1994. "For two weeks, I or another itinerant teacher would teach in different cities," he said. "Churches would have everything organized and there would be twenty to eighty students waiting for us. It was also very much appreciated by missionaries, as we gave them complementary Bible teaching on top of what they had managed to fit into their busy schedules."

In 1994, ABI moved to a base in Durres, where it rented a school building. It started residential programmes in September 1996 and bought the building in 1997, helped by ECM, which gave 50,000 dollars. "Our Bible school was geared towards church leaders, with one week in school and two weeks out," continued Frans. "This way they could still lead their churches while being students. Some of them were already pastoring churches, while others assisted missionaries in doing so."

Berti and fifteen other key Albanians were the first to be invited to enrol for a three-year course for these new Christians. For one week in every three, Berti lived in Durres, which was an hour and a half's drive away, and attended the lectures. The other two weeks he spent time writing essays and reading the textbooks, as well as fitting in family and work, plus leading the church in Lushnjë. Frans particularly remembers Berti Dosti, who was in the first group of students and was older than the others. "He was great in helping us to understand Albanian culture," he recalled.

It was a big commitment for Berti and the other Albanians. No one knew how costly it would be two years later in 1997, when anarchy gripped the country and gunmen controlled the streets of Albania.

Chapter 19

1997 – AN *ANNUS HORRIBILIS*

If the new Albanian church expected a few quiet years in which it could consolidate, nothing could have been further from the truth. The year 1997 was a baptism of fire, with an economic scandal bringing down the government, a civil war, anarchy on the streets as citizens carried guns for protection, and most of the missionaries having to leave the country for their own safety.

If the new church could survive all that, then it could face the future with confidence. As the Albanian Christians look back now, many would say that year was a turning point. Between 1994 and 1996 there had been rapid economic growth in Albania, with money coming into the country, particularly from Albanians living abroad. People were keen to make up for years of austerity, and were tempted to invest in financial institutions offering unrealistically high rates of returns. To keep these high rates of return, banking "pyramids" developed, and new investors had to be found so their capital could meet existing liabilities. It is believed that up to two-thirds of the population, including many Christians, invested in what is known as Ponzi schemes, with some even selling their home so they could invest more.

The pyramid schemes, offering high interest rates, were a temptation to all. Berti sometimes tried, and failed, to persuade people not to sell their homes as they came to the solicitor's office with their documents to finalize the sale. "Why are you selling? Are you doing the right thing?" Berti would ask, but by then they were all determined to go ahead with the deal. Even members of the church put money into the schemes. Tatjana confessed she had put a small amount in, without telling Berti, when she and the staff at the court decided to invest one day. Even Berti, trying to help his brother, had opened a small account.

In October 1996 the Albanian government ignored the International Monetary Fund's warnings as investors began to lose confidence and withdraw money, and financial institutions began to collapse. In November the Albanian president, Sali Berisha, went on TV to try to allay people's fears and told them that Albanian money was the cleanest in the world. That only worried the people even more. They thought somehow that the government was behind the pyramid scheme. On 4 and 5 January 1997 there were long queues as people tried to withdraw their money. The next day the financial scheme leaders disappeared, the system collapsed, and thousands of angry Albanians took to the streets after losing all their cash. It is estimated that the Albanian people lost the equivalent of 1.2 billion dollars.

But not quite everyone lost money. Alma and her husband Drini invested some money in the pyramid scheme and a few months later decided to buy a house. They withdrew the money – and the profits – just in time.

Eventually, most of the pyramid scheme leaders were arrested by Interpol, tried, and then imprisoned, but the vast majority of the Albanian people didn't get their money back.

Things then came to a head, politically. One of the first towns where trouble erupted was Lushnjë, which was where the pyramid scheme had begun. On Saturday 25 January crowds began to vent their anger against the government, which they felt should have protected them. Enraged investors went on the rampage, even attacking the Foreign Minister Tritan Shehu when he visited the town. When Berti made his way to church at the top of the dental building the next day for the 11 a.m. service there were thousands of people in the town centre. Some were there out of curiosity, but many wanted revenge on the government and were systematically setting fire to all the municipal buildings, including the court.

Berti wondered what he could do. He thought he would have to cancel the church service, as he didn't think anyone would dare turn up. However, he thought he would make his way to the top floor of the dentist's building and see if anyone was there. When he arrived, he was amazed: the church was full, with thirty people present. For the second time that morning Berti wondered what he could do. He decided to change the agreed service and lead a prayer meeting instead.

Outside, the people of Lushnjë were on their knees economically, while inside, some of the Christians of Lushnja were on their knees spiritually. As the town's government buildings burned, so the believers prayed. At the same time as the prayer meeting, thousands of people were clashing with riot police and setting government buildings alight in Tirana and other towns and cities across the country.

After an hour, the Lushnjë church meeting finished and the Christians carefully made their way home, through even bigger crowds. As Berti and Tatjana picked their way through the mob, the people didn't realize what a brave service the couple had done already for the town. Knowing there was going to be trouble, Tatjana and others had got up early, gone to the courts in a car with her boss, entered the offices and taken away all the important documents for safekeeping – and all by 7 a.m. Berti had done the same by collecting the vital documents from his solicitor's office and storing them in a safe place.

During February, thousands of citizens all over the country continued to gather daily to protest, and by March it had become even more violent. Rioters took control of the town of Sarande, seizing weapons, including Kalashnikovs and even tanks, from police headquarters and army barracks, as the local military stood by and watched. Most of the southern half of the country fell into the hands of rebels and criminal gangs, while more than 10,000 people fled to Italy, causing a government crisis in Rome. Several high Albanian government officials, including the Defence Minister Safet Zhulali, fled abroad. On 2 March, President Berisha declared a state of emergency as foreign embassies began to send their nationals back home for safety.[1]

"It was anarchy for the first few months," said Berti. "It was very dangerous to go out on the streets, as there were even teenagers with guns, and many, many people were killed. Schools and factories were closed, and people couldn't go to work, even if they had a job to go to." Many Christians in Berti's church asked him: should Christians carry guns? Many of them felt unsafe without a weapon, but Berti, who had been trained to use weapons in the army, always advised his church members against it.

However, the problems were brought home to the Christians a few weeks later when a couple of armed gunmen threatened about a dozen of them while they were having a Bible study. The first time, they took the speakers from the church room, and Berti saw no point in trying to stop them. He had to caution a couple of teenagers in the church who wanted to get some guns and go after them. Over the next few weeks, the gunmen came back and stripped the room of everything, including even the radiators.

Berti and the worshippers realized that they had to find a safer building. A believer offered his home on the fourth floor of an apartment block, and they met there until the political situation settled down. The roads were dangerous too. Gangs were stationed along them like modern-day highwaymen, to hold up and rob people in cars – and even on buses.

Despite the dangers, Berti was still determined to continue his Bible course at the Albanian Bible Institute, and he continued to go regularly by car to Durres. "I was nervous," he admitted, "and Tatjana was always glad to see me back home. But God protected me, and my car was never attacked, although I did see people who were."

An even bigger challenge was when ECM delivered 24,000 dollars to Berti, who was the leading pastor for all the Way of Peace churches. This was to buy a house which was to be the new church in Fier. But how was Berti to get the money to Fier, an hour's drive away, when there was no guarantee he could get there safely? Even the banks weren't considered a safe place, so he couldn't deposit the money there. Using his military expertise and planning, he hit upon a solution. One night Berti reversed his van as close as he could to his apartment stairs. To the outsider it looked as though he was repairing the back doors of his van. In reality, he was unscrewing the linings so he could hide the money inside the door. Next day he drove down to Fier to hand over the money to the owner of the house that the church had bought, and returned with the signed contract. "I was relieved to get back home that day," recalled Berti. Where the house owner put the money, Berti doesn't know. However, he said many people dug holes and hid money in their gardens.

Although life was dangerous for Albanians, it was even worse for the missionaries, who were obvious targets, as they stood out from the crowds and had more money than the locals. With a heavy heart, in March 1997, ECM and other Christian organizations pulled out most of their missionaries and workers for their own safety. Of the 600 or so missionaries in the country, about 550 left, all of them worried about how the new, young Albanian church would survive. Fortunately, many were able to return three months later.

Stephen Bell recalled the terrible times as the missionaries escaped by whatever way possible. Some were taken by helicopter to Rome, some drove to Greece, while Gani and Adile Smolica plus their four children flew to Turkey. Stephen Bell said of his family, "We became refugees, fleeing explosive Albania on 11 March. Many missionaries left by helicopter, in awful circumstances, but we went in style on seemingly the last car ferry across the Adriatic to Italy, even stopping off for a family pizza at a restaurant on the way to the Durres port!"

Stephen, worried about the church, flew back the following month. He said in a letter home to his parents, "I was able to be in Albania from April 17 until May 11. I went alone by plane so as not to risk the car being stolen in chaotic Albania. However, it was not as bad as I thought it could be. Sure, to an outsider's eye it was mayhem, but those who have experienced February and March are thankful for small mercies. There is shooting at night, but this is mostly friendly fire, i.e. neighbours shooting into the sky, declaring to potential thieves that they are armed and no easy prey.

"There are people being killed, alas, daily, but these casualties can be put into three categories: a. Mafia robbers fighting with other robbers and Mafia; b. Revenge killings, often Mafia-linked; c. Accidents, usually involving children.

"Whilst these are terrible, they do not put innocent people and missionaries at risk, so there is very little looting and now no highway robbery, which did happen during March. Of course in the 'rebel' south (Vlorë, Sarande and Gjirokastër) anything still goes."

Stephen said he was encouraged by the way the churches had survived, and in some cases grown. He said, "During my three-week visit I had two main goals – to show my face as much as possible and to go to as many meetings as I could to prepare the churches to be more independent and able to face the future, maybe without missionaries. In Fier numbers were up, and I noticed they were generally enthusiastic, giving friends and neighbours hope in a sad world. I spent a couple of Wednesday nights at Berti's house, going to two Bible studies. They had done well: the fellowship was enjoying its most successful spell during its four years in existence. New people had come and the challenge is now to teach them. Berti was very encouraged, although he is under a great personal workload and gets up at 5 a.m."

Although Berti had heard of a few churches closing, some Albanian believers, who had not done any studying, volunteered to help the leaders. As a result of people being thrown in at the deep end spiritually, the churches had grown, attracting visitors worried about the political situation. Berti said, "It was a real test for the Albanian leaders and believers, and overall they did well."

At the end of April, Stephen visited two missionaries in Vlorë who had decided not to leave Albania: Peter Hoffmann and Mark

Nyberg. Peter was helping with the Way of Peace fellowship there, and Mark was the director of the orphanage. Both recounted harrowing details of what life had been like during the past two months. When their year's supply of food had been looted and they had only one week's supply left, they had no choice but to try to get to the Greek border, three hours' drive away. There they could buy badly-needed supplies for the sixty-five orphans and pick up the 27,000 dollars for the fifty workers, who had not been paid for three months.

"As they travelled they were held up and threatened by armed assailants on numerous occasions, but they got through," said Stephen. "Believers from the church slept at the two town orphanages and also at the missionaries' houses, keeping armed guard." Stephen had an unusual group to protect his own house. He and Tabita had left in March, and soon afterwards robbers arrived. Then the "Triangle" sprang into action. The "Triangle" consisted of three elderly neighbours – Mihallaqi, who lived opposite Stephen, and two sixty-year-olds, Zani, next door, and Tarif, on the other side of the Bells – who arrived on the scene complete with Kalashnikovs and challenged the would-be thieves.

For the next four weeks they guarded the house, shooting into the sky in time-honoured style, while believers from the church occasionally slept there. When the Bell family returned to their home, they invited the "Triangle" members into their garden for sausage and chips to mark their appreciation. "They vowed no thief would threaten me or Tabita or Sheona again," recalled Stephen.

There were also other lighter moments for those left behind, as Mark recalls. Vlorë, where the orphanage was, was firmly under the control of a local Mafia "godfather" and a few hundred of his armed men. Previously, Mark had been having problems from a neighbour who had threatened him with a Kalashnikov, objecting to an extension the orphanage was planning to build. Coincidentally, fifteen minutes later, after a difficult meeting with the neighbour, the Mafia godfather came along with an entourage of ten cars, bursting with twenty men plus Kalashnikovs, bombs, and grenades. The Mafia leader offered Mark 1,500 eggs to feed the children, as he was obviously pleased with the work the orphanage was doing, and commented that if he had any problems he should phone him directly.

As the godfather departed, Mark told the workers to spread the word that the Mafia leader was very upset that the neighbours wanted to hinder the building of the new extension. Within ten minutes, a rather sweating neighbour ran up to Mark, saying that he now had no objection to any building and he would be willing to help with the project in any way possible.

Meanwhile, worried that this anarchy would lead to mass emigration to Western Europe, the United Nations authorized an international military force of 7,000 soldiers under Greek and Italian leadership, codenamed Operation Sunrise, to direct relief and restore order. They arrived on 15 April, in the same month that a transitional government was formed. Elections were held in the following June and July: President Berisha was voted out of office and the Socialists took power, with Rexhep Mejdani elected president. By August all UN forces had left Albania, and by the autumn the new government reckoned it controlled most, if not all, of the country again.

The only problem was that an estimated 3,000,000 weapons stolen from the army then made their way north into the hands of the underground Kosovo Liberation Army (KLA), which was fighting a major guerrilla campaign against the Yugoslav army units and Serbian police. The repercussions of that move were to have a major impact on Albania in the following eighteen months.

Chapter 20

VICTORY AFTER A YEAR OF ANARCHY

At the end of 1997, the country began to return to normal, but there were huge economic problems, with high unemployment and many young people, including Christians, emigrating to find jobs. Berti knew that Albania couldn't afford to lose its young people, and so the church came up with the idea of starting a school. It would serve the local church, employ Christians, giving them an incentive to stay in the country, and teach young people English, which would give them a better chance of finding work. It would also give the church respect and a good reputation within the community.

With the help of ECM workers Stephen Bell, Murray Cotter, and Douglas Livingston, Albanian Christians started English classes in Lushnjë, Fier, and Patos, calling them Victory Schools. They appointed a board in each of the three towns so that the classes could be run professionally and fulfil all legal requirements, and, most importantly, would be recognized by the Albanian authorities.

The first class began in Fier in September 1997 with eight students. A month later the first class started in Lushnjë after a believer allowed the first floor of her two-storey house to be used. At the first lesson were five pupils, who each paid ten dollars a month. ECM provided a TV, video recorder, tables, and desks, while the Abraham Lincoln Foundation of Albania provided books, equipment, and other educational material, as well as giving advice on how to set up and run the school.

"Although I had no experience in managing a school, I did not see it as a business but as a service to God," said Berti. "I work for the school and God grows it." And the school certainly grew. It was a credit to Berti's character that he was flexible and willing to have a go at a completely new project. Within a year it expanded, with three teachers using all three rooms on the first floor and teaching nine hour-long classes, each with a maximum of ten pupils.

As further premises were needed, one of the Christian teachers, Elsa Ndrecka, mentioned she was friends with a girl whose family lived in a large house 200 metres away from the classrooms. The family invited Berti and Elsa to look round the house. As they climbed the stairs to second floor of the large building, Berti turned to Elsa and said, "One day all this will be ours." He was correct: the building became the Victory School, but it would be another ten years before his prophecy came true. In the meantime, the girl's father, Loni, let them rent two rooms to provide a fourth and fifth classroom.

Many Albanians were desperate to learn English, and through Berti's leadership skills and the school's growing reputation for high standards and honesty, numbers grew every year. Berti insisted the school paid all its high taxes in full, unlike some businesses in Albania.

All the students were prepared for Level 1 and Level 2 examinations, and those who passed were presented with a certificate from the Lincoln Foundation, which was recognized by the Albanian Ministry of Employment. In some Albanian schools it was said that some teachers failed to teach their students well during the day in order to persuade them to pay for private tuition in the teachers' homes in the evening. It was also claimed that some teachers needed to be bribed to give students the pass grades that would get them into higher education.

By 2000, the school employed its fifth teacher, Alma Syla, who had certainly come into the profession the hard way.

When many Albanians left the country in 1990, attracted by better-paid jobs abroad, there were many job vacancies in professions, including teaching. Eighteen-year-old Alma had wanted to be a teacher since she was a child and she decided to apply, even though she hadn't any qualifications. To her delight, she was offered a job, but it was in a remote village. To get to the school, in Spolet, it meant catching the 6:30 a.m. bus from Lushnjë for an hour's journey, then a 45-minute walk through two villages to the school, where she started teaching at 8:30 a.m. and finished at 1:30 p.m. Then she had to repeat the journey, arriving home at 3 p.m. After a meal and a rest, she started her own studies and preparing the next day's lessons, until 10:30 p.m., depending on whether there were any power cuts, which were frequent in those days.

Alma had applied for a scholarship to study part-time at a university in Tirana. Although a few thousand students had entered, Alma was one of only 100 selected, and in the autumn of 1990 she began a diploma in Albanian language and literature. Soon after she started, the students went on strike, on 8 December 1990. The government responded by closing the universities and didn't reopen them until the following April, which affected Alma's studies. Berti was also impacted, as he was ordered to join the Rapid Defence Force in Kavaja to deal with the civil unrest.

Meanwhile, Alma had to concentrate on her teaching and had to put back her studies for a term, as she couldn't take her exams because of the closure of the university. In 1991, Alma moved to a school nearer home. Fier-Seman was only an hour's bus ride away, with no walk at the other end. However, over the next few years, life became even more hectic as she continued her teaching and her studies in the evening.

In 1994, Alma married Drini, who ran his own electrical business in Lushnjë, and the following year she gave birth to her first daughter, Sabrina. As if that was not enough, in June she started to learn English at a neighbour's house. Their twenty-year-old daughter, Enkeleda, taught Alma English while Alma's mother looked after Sabrina. "Enkeleda was very hard-working but very poor," recalled Alma, "but she was so happy and always singing. When I asked her why she was always singing, she said it was because she was a Christian." This started many discussions between Enkeleda and Alma during the English conversation classes and led to them eventually praying together with Enkeleda's mother. "That was the start of my Christian journey," said Alma.

At the same time, Alma became very friendly with Elsa, a Christian teacher at her school. They began sitting together on the bus and spent the hour's journey in prayer and studying the Bible together. Elsa gave Alma her first Bible, which she still uses today. The pair taught at a school for fourteen- to eighteen-year-olds, where most of the villagers were from an Orthodox background. However, when the two teachers spoke about their faith to the students, the director called them into his office and banned them from talking about religion. Even so, the students wanted to continue the discussions, and one of the parents let them use his dusty old office in a little-used house in the village.

Alma and Elsa accepted his offer, cleaned and painted the room, and brought in bricks and wood to provide benches.

Every Thursday at 2 p.m., after school had finished, the two teachers went to their new office and taught Christianity for an hour. "We had up to sixty students," said Alma, "and though the parents knew what was going on, they didn't mind and even welcomed us into their homes." After two years, Elsa moved to another job. "I cried on the bus when I heard the news," said Alma, who continued at that school for two years before getting a job in Lushnjë. She worked there in the mornings, and in 2000 started teaching at the Victory School in the afternoons, where numbers were now more than 100.

To cope with the increasing numbers, Berti again went to the owner, Loni, to ask for more rooms. Loni happily agreed to rent the school another three rooms because now only he and his wife were left at home, as their two daughters and son had emigrated to America. By 2004, Loni and his wife decided to join their children in the States and they told Berti, "The building is all yours." They allowed the school to rent the whole building and develop it as they wished for 600 dollars a month. Berti, with his amazing vision and ability to plan ahead, set about finding the money to allow the church to buy the property. Three years later the building was bought for 210,000 dollars, with the money raised from school profits, donations, and a large loan from ECM. In the meantime, with the help of builders and church volunteers, they added an extra floor to provide three more classrooms so they could move the school to one site. Even after this, the small church still had the vision for further projects.

Finding a job was still a problem for the students, so in 2004 the school began two new ventures. First, it introduced two computer classes five times a week. Berti persuaded Charles Bell, from Calvary Church in California, USA, to help them by sending teams to Lushnjë to teach English and computer studies, as well as providing cash, laptops, digital projectors, and advice on training. Second, when the charity Hope for Albania, a Christian relief agency based in the Netherlands, provided Berti with six sewing machines, the school decided to start a tailoring class, as it was even harder for women to find work. A room was set aside in the school to provide free two-hour lessons twice a week for a three-month course. It proved a great success, and more than sixty women completed the training. Many then found work and joined the church. One of those women was Alma's mother, Ervehe Tabaku.

By 2007, there were nearly 300 students, but not all of them were fee-paying students. The school was aware that many children could not afford to come, so it introduced a scholarship scheme. More than eighty students from poor backgrounds have taken advantage of it.

Berti said there were many joys in running both the school and the church. One of those was to see students organizing shows, concerts, and celebrations in the church, which would attract their parents and friends. "The church became known in the community because of the growing reputation of the Victory School," said Berti. However, there were frustrations as well. "One of those was living in a town where the young people go away at eighteen, either to university or abroad, and few return," said Berti. "Because of that we are always looking for new leaders in the church and new teachers in the school." Berti knew that from personal experience with his daughter Alta and his son Dorian, who both went away to university.

When Alta began to learn English at school, she helped

Berti to prepare and translate the Sunday school material. As she got older, she started taking the classes on her own and then translating Biblical commentaries to help her father with his sermons. When there was an English-speaking preacher in church, Alta was the interpreter. Later she led the teenage Bible study in church. Then she accompanied Berti when he travelled abroad, as he told churches about the work in Albania. "She became my right hand: she was superb," said Berti.

Alta also helped Berti at the Victory School. When she went to university in 2001 to study English and become a teacher, she still supported the school and the church work when she came home. Unlike many youngsters, Alta did come back to Lushnjë, and she helped more with the school management. When she married Lenci, Berti was so impressed with his new son-in-law that he appointed him assistant pastor at the church and course director at the Victory School, jobs he did for five years. He said, "I am very grateful to God for giving me Alta and Lenci. They have been great supporters in my ministry, and my life and I were thrilled when they were the first couple to be married at the Way of Peace Church, on 11 September 2005."

Another great helper was Berti's son Dorian, who has been going to the church since he was five years old. "His great hobby is computers, and God has used his gift for the Way of Peace Church and the Victory School," said Berti. The school and church never needed to hire a computer technician, as Dorian took care of everything. Even when Dorian went to university in Tirana to study computer sciences, he came home many weekends to check the computer systems in the church and the school.

Berti could never solve the drain of young people completely, although the Victory School also helped some to get local employment. Two of the pupils, who had learnt English at the school, are now teachers there. Ingrida Nako studied English at Elbasan University before she returned to Lushnjë in 2005 and got a job at the school. She is now engaged to Ledion, whom she met at Victory School, and who now runs his own bar in town. Erisa Xhaja, who spent two and a half years at Victory School being taught by Alma among others, left to study English, German, and Spanish in Tirana. The day she arrived back home in Lushnjë, her mother said she had seen an advertisement for a teacher at the Victory School, and within two weeks of returning Erisa was given a job back at her old school.

Berti never allowed anything to faze him, as he was totally committed to doing what God wanted. Still, it was quite an achievement for a former electrician and kiosk owner to open a school and take on the financial responsibility of running it without any training, as well as overseeing a church at the same time. However, the church was quite a way from the school, so Berti was always travelling between the two. He knew he could solve the problem of being in different places as pastor and school principal, but it was another ambitious and costly scheme, which he would shortly put to both the church and the school.

Chapter 21

COPING WITH HALF A MILLION REFUGEES

After the baptism of fire with the pyramid selling scandal in 1997, the young Albanian church might have thought things would calm down. But within months, the church faced a different but just as serious challenge, when more than half a million refugees, the equivalent of 15 per cent of Albania's population, fled into the country from the war in Kosovo in late 1998 and early 1999.

The Kosovo question had been a problem throughout Albania's history. Following the First Balkan War of 1912, the Treaty of London recognized Kosovo as part of Serbia. It also recognized Albania as an independent sovereign state, even though more than half the Albanian population were left outside the new state's borders. Many of these Albanians were now in Kosovo, which in 1918 became part of the newly-formed Kingdom of Serbs, Croats and Slovenes, later named Yugoslavia.

After the Second World War, under President Tito, Kosovo slowly achieved more independence, and by 1974 it was practically self-governing. The Albanian curriculum was introduced in schools, and the authorities even began using Enver Hoxha textbooks. However, in the 1980s, tensions increased, with the Kosovar Albanians wanting to become a republic within Yugoslavia, but they didn't want to join with Albania because of its poorer living standards and its Stalinist government. On the other hand, the Kosovo Serbs wanted closer ties with Serbia. By August 1987, Kosovo Serbs felt the Communist authorities in Belgrade were neglecting them, and when a rising politician, Slobodan Milosevic, arrived in Kosovo and appealed to Serb nationalism, he was treated as a hero. By the end of the year he was in charge of the Serbian government, and he later imposed martial law after mass demonstrations by Kosovar Albanians had been put down with the loss of life in 1989. The protesters were objecting to a Serbian referendum, brought in by force, which drastically reduced Kosovo's autonomy. Education in Albanian was withdrawn, at Prishtina University education in the Albanian language was abolished, and 200,000 Albanian workers were sacked in two months.

Following the end of Communism, relations between the two communities deteriorated further as the Serbs took control and many Albanians lost their jobs. Then thousands of Serb refugees from Croatia settled in Kosovo in 1995. By late 1997, the situation escalated into war, with many Kosovar Albanians killed. Many others were forced from their homes at gunpoint, with most of them fleeing over the border into Albania. The Albanian Foreign Ministry called for NATO military intervention to stop the fighting, and eventually all sides were invited to an international conference in Rambouillet, France, in February 1999. Following the breakdown of talks, NATO forces launched a bombing campaign against Yugoslavia from 24 March until 10 June to force Milosevic to return to the negotiating table and withdraw his forces from Kosovo.[1]

With half a million refugees streaming into the country,

Albania's fragile infrastructure collapsed, leaving its government and the international humanitarian agencies unable to cope.

However, help arrived from an unexpected quarter. The Albanian Evangelical Alliance, (the Vëllazëria Ungjillore e Shqipërise or VUSh in Albanian), stepped in. It had been set up in October 1993 as an umbrella organization for the evangelical churches and drew inspiration from an evangelical brotherhood founded in 1892 by Gjerasim Qiraiazi. Born on 18 October 1858 in Ternova, Macedonia, Gjerasim was an evangelical preacher and educationalist in Albania who was captured by brigands and held prisoner for six months, was publicly criticized by the Greek Orthodox Church, and survived an assassination attempt. On Monday 14 November 1892, Gjerasim founded a national society, the Vëllazëria Ungjillore, to unite the people to work for the good of the nation. He was elected the first president of the society, but he died just over a year later on 2 January 1894. He was only thirty-five years old.[2]

With a network of 120 churches across the country, VUSh volunteered to organize and run transit centres in every major town and city. At the time, its president was Berti, who had been appointed in October 1997 for a three-year term. "When I was at the Albanian Bible Institute a group from VUSh came to meet me," recalled Berti. "They said many people had recommended me to be the next VUSh president, and they asked me what I thought about it." He added, "I was speechless for a few moments, but as I am a person who enjoys a challenge I immediately thought it was God's plan for me to contribute to the Albanian church and I accepted it. I was totally honoured and privileged. I had never thought my service to God would have so much effect on my life and other people's lives, and that others believed I could do this important role."

As well as his involvement in meetings in Albania, Berti represented the country abroad at Balkan, European, and world conferences, and went to Amsterdam for a Billy Graham conference in 2000. "It was a privilege to travel to these conferences, as it gave me the opportunity to say what God was doing in Albania, that the new churches were starting to grow and that the country was now open as a mission field," said Berti. However, within eighteen months of Berti taking office, he and VUSh were in the national spotlight because of the Kosovo crisis. "We were totally unprepared for this and we had no experience in dealing with it," he said. "It was a very difficult role for me, as I had two duties. First, in Tirana, as VUSh president, I had to manage the situation for the evangelical Albanian churches, and second, in Lushnjë, as a pastor, I had to oversee the situation there. It was like a war on two fronts."

So how did they deal with the situation? First, in Tirana the executive committee of VUSh organized an emergency meeting, where they fasted and prayed. Second, they set up a headquarters to manage the situation and contacted all the churches, offering them VUSh's support and asking them what their needs were. Third, they launched a website to communicate with all the churches and tell them what was going on. Finally, they sent an SOS to churches and organizations abroad, asking them to help with prayer, money, and emergency supplies.

In Lushnjë, Berti, like many pastors, challenged his church by asking the members, "Are you ready to help our brothers and sisters in need?" They were, and they rose to the challenge brilliantly.

More than 5,000 refugees came to Lushnjë in March 1999.

The first wave was people who were coming to stay with relatives. All the churches in the town responded, giving their own food and blankets, before the international aid arrived, including financial help from ECM.

Alma and her husband Drini, whose parents are Kosovans, lived in a small rented two-roomed flat with their two children. When Drini's relatives arrived, they stored all the furniture in one room, while twelve of them lived in the other one. "Each morning we piled up all the mattresses on the one bed to make room for us all," recalled Alma. There was no bathroom or running water in their sixth-floor flat. For water, they had to go down to the tap on the ground floor and carry it back up six flights of stairs. For a bath, they had to go back down to the ground floor, cross the street, and go up to the fourth floor of a block of flats nearby to use the bathroom at Alma's parents' house. "Despite twelve of us living so close together, none of us got any infections," said Alma.

However, the refugees kept coming into Albania. In the second wave, refugees without relatives in Lushnjë came into the town, camping on the sides of the roads, and local people took complete strangers into their homes. Even though many of the Lushnjë people were very poor, and were still recovering from losing their money in the pyramid scandal, they gave so much to help the refugees.

Civic officials in Lushnjë called a Council of Emergency and invited all the institutions, organizations, and churches to decide how to pool their resources. A new board was set up for the town, with Berti representing the six evangelical churches. With his military, emergency planning and organizational skills, he was the ideal candidate, and he immediately submitted a plan of action on behalf of the churches to the Council of Emergency.

The board decided to divide Lushnja into zones, with the churches looking after one zone. Berti arranged to rent four shops, paid for by the churches and staffed by local Christians, to provide free bread for the refugees. The board also hired a depot to store all the international aid coming into Lushnjë. However, within three weeks, they had to find another depot as it was too small.

In Tirana, Gani, Adile, and their four children, who were all Kosovar Albanians, had thirty relatives staying in their two-bedroom house for a time. "When the relatives returned to Kosovo the house seemed quite large with just five of us in," he joked.

Further south in Albania, Stephen wrote home to England to try to tell family and friends what the situation was like. "We alone in Fier (population 70,000) have more than 12,000 refugees, and I believe our number will increase to more than 30,000 as Kosovo empties and Albania fills," he reported. "The four evangelical churches in Fier have united in their efforts to distribute aid and love to these poor people. We started with £300, which we collected among ourselves, and are now expecting generous gifts from British, French, German, and American Christians. They have sent money and trucks, which should begin to arrive next week. We have bought clothes and food for about 1,000 Kosovans who are living in 'institutions'. These are the fourth and fifth floors of the officers' houses, where 242 people are living on one floor under our rented meeting hall. I have also visited 160 people at the 'Base of Tubes', where three large families are living in an open barn about the size of a five-a-side football pitch.

"The family of Ibrahim, a very good friend of Shau-Ping, my Chinese Christian friend in my Prishtina days, had to travel for five days in an open lorry with seventy others. They even had to pass beheaded corpses on the way. I am now trying to get them accommodation in Fier, but it is a soul-destroying task. On the one hand, there are the Albanians who want £220 a month rent from a family of eight. On the other hand there is a couple in Fier with three children who are living in the reception area of a disused and derelict cinema and are willing to move up to a windowless attic to allow these poor Kosovans to move into their space. This family are so poor, but they are willing to give all to people poorer than they are – and for free. Truly, this mess brings out the best and worst in people."

Many individuals and aid organizations went to help the Albanian church cope with the Kosovan crisis. One of those sent out by ECM was Arthur Prescott, whose business skills proved invaluable. After taking early retirement, Arthur, an electrical engineer, joined ECM, first as a volunteer and then as a full-time worker. He went out in May 1999 to help the churches in Fier and Lushnjë with the refugees.

"For five weeks I looked after the warehouse in Fier," recalled Arthur. "Stephen Bell and the local Christians, including Berti in Lushnjë, had done such a great job that many of the larger professional aid agencies were envious of what had already been achieved before they arrived. But even they were overwhelmed by the money, food, and clothes flooding in from the West. When I arrived in Fier, Stephen gave me several large bags full of currencies from all over the world and asked me to get them changed into Albanian lek (the local currency), which was quite a challenge since there were no operating banks. All money had to be changed using one of the many money-changers in the town square – their sleight of hand was something to be admired."

On 10 June 1999 the war ended with the Kumanovo agreement, by which the administration of Kosovo was transferred to the United Nations. The next day, a NATO-led Kosovo Force entered the area to provide security to the UN mission in Kosovo. After seventy-eight days of war, about half of the 200,000 Kosovo Serbs left Kosovo in the summer of 1999, while the ethnic Albanians, ignoring UN warnings of danger, returned to their homes in Kosovo. There was a huge line of traffic as the grateful Kosovar Albanians headed home on whatever transport they could find, ranging from cars, lorries, and tractors to any agricultural vehicle that could move.

As the Christians still had some money and goods left over once the refugees had returned home, Arthur and Stephen decided to hire a lorry, fill it with the remaining food and clothes, plus fridges and cookers, and return with the refugees to Kosovo. With a local driver and an interpreter, Arthur began the ten-hour journey from Fier in southern Albania to Peja in Kosovo over the mountain passes. "In those days," said Arthur, "it was a very poor road with no signposts and many obstacles, so it was a treacherous and hairy trip – but quite an adventure."

Arthur went to Peja because they had contacts there through Gani's family. When they arrived, they were shocked by what greeted them. The streets were in total darkness, apart from a few flames and torches. Many of the buildings owned by Kosovar Albanians had been destroyed, while nearby were the smouldering homes of Serbs who had fled as the Kosovar Albanians returned home. "Whole streets were full of rubble three feet high and it was very difficult to get around," said Arthur. "The Serbians had first shelled the civilian homes and businesses, and then had gone down the streets firebombing every Kosovar Albanian house; these had collapsed inwardly, so they were just piles of rubble as well. On top of that the Italian peace-keeping troops warned about mines and firebombs that hadn't been detonated."

Arthur spent two weeks there, delivering the goods, talking to the UN and aid agencies, filming, and planning his next trip. He returned a few months later when ECM launched a long-term project to help rebuild homes and support families in Peja, Prishtina, and nearby villages. "The people were just in despair: we had to help," said Arthur.

Looking back a decade later, Berti said that according to VUSh's own statistics, during the first two weeks of the crisis the evangelicals, who total fewer than half a per cent of the population, dealt with nearly 80 per cent of the refugees. They ensured they were met, fed, registered, and sent out to families or camps to be looked after. "We are still amazed what God did through His churches in Albania," said Berti. "It was a big test for the church and they coped well. It was an excellent experience for them. A lot of friendships were made, some became Christians, and the church was thanked on TV, by aid organizations, government officials, and even by the President for its help."

After the crisis was over President Rexhep Mejdani said, "I wish to acknowledge the evangelical believers of Albania for the dedication and service rendered to tens of thousands of refugees during one of the most difficult chapters in the history of our nation. Throughout the country these believers exemplified faith in action through their practical application of the Golden Rule, 'Do unto others as you would have them do unto you.'"[3]

Chapter 22

I WILL BUILD MY CHURCH (MATTHEW 16:18)

It was in early 1998 that Berti decided the church had to look for new premises. There was no point in going back to the dental building where they had had the problems with the armed raid and other thefts. For the last few months, they had been meeting in a believer's apartment, but it was very cramped, and Berti decided it was only fair that the church should move.

It was Berti's friend Ladi and ECM Eastern Europe director Stuart Rowell who came up with an unusual solution. In Albania, it is traditional that when a son gets married, his parents give him land to build a house. So Ladi, who had married in 1987, had built a two-storey house, which included a large flat roof and balcony, on his parents' land next to his and Berti's kiosk. Stuart, who had trained as a construction engineer before joining ECM, suggested, rather ingeniously, putting a roof over the flat area. Ladi could then rent that part of his house to the church, to which he agreed.

While they were planning the "Balcony Church", as the believers called it, Stephen Bell came to preach at the Way of Peace Church and took as his theme the Old Testament book of Nehemiah. There, the prophet had challenged the Jews to rebuild in fifty-two days the walls of Jerusalem, which were in a desolate state after King Nebuchadnezzar had destroyed the city and taken most of the Jews into exile in the sixth century BC. Berti then called on the Lushnjë Christians to build their church on the balcony in fifty-two days – and they rose to the challenge. ECM loaned the church 5,000 dollars, and together with other donations they began building in May. A church in Tirana had a business producing corrugated iron, and Berti negotiated a good price for the roof material. Ladi had a friend, Agim, who was a professional builder, and he agreed to oversee the project. Every church member gave of his or her time and talents. Berti did the electrics, while some of the teenagers went to school in the morning and spent their afternoons labouring on the balcony. Meanwhile, youth in the church formed a long line to pass the bricks and cement up to the builders on the balcony. By 1 June, the "Balcony Church" was completed, fifty-two days after the project was launched. Again, church members had responded superbly.

"It was a great team effort and I was really grateful for all their help," said Berti. Stuart Rowell added, "I was really impressed by Berti. His organizational skills are phenomenal. He is always working on a plethora of activities and he gets people working. He has a large vision and has an ability to persevere, even with limited resources, as this project showed."

On Sunday 7 June 1998, the church celebrated with its first service in the new building.

At the same time, Berti completed his three-year course at the Albanian Bible Institute and Stephen suggested he became the full-time pastor. Berti knew it would be difficult financially if he gave up his job as a notary's assistant. In addition, he didn't receive a pension from the army, as he had completed only eleven years' military service, not the minimum fifteen years. But the church was growing, and Berti decided to talk to the members about having a full-time pastor.

The church agreed that they wanted a full-time pastor, and that it should be Berti. In the autumn, Berti resigned from his job and agreed to sell his share in the kiosk business, although Ladi kindly gave him a third of the kiosk profits for the next two years to help him financially. He also returned the capital Berti had put into the business. Now he had the kiosk money, Berti decided he wouldn't take a salary as pastor, as he was already being paid as principal of the Victory School.

On Sunday 4 October 1998, more than 100 people packed into the "Balcony Church" to see Berti appointed pastor. Among the guests were Stephen, Gani, Frans Blok of the Albanian Bible Institute, Murray Cotter from the Way of Peace Church in Patos, Ray Nye, a pastor from the UK and a friend of ECM, plus family, friends, and members of the church. "It was a very emotional moment," said Berti. "Although I was excited, I was also a little fearful of the future. It was a big challenge, and I was concerned whether I would be a good pastor."

Berti was very successful as a pastor and found the job very satisfying. However, as well as the joys, there were also a few difficulties. One of them was trying to get more men to come to the church. Berti believed this reluctance was due to the role of men in Albanian society: men are the head of the family and they are highly respected because "they bring the bread onto the family table". But he added that throughout their lives men were expected to obey their parents and accept their way of life, including religion. Men were responsible if any member followed a different course to their ancestors' religion and traditions, such as becoming a Christian. In addition, he said, men could not afford to lose face with friends or family, so they would follow the trend and not go against peer pressure. An example of this would be going to church, which would be considered odd by their friends. Berti knew that Albanian men have an inner personal pride that stopped them committing themselves to any religion that was new to their mindset. Another problem was that some who came from an Orthodox background said they were Christians even though they never went to church. To try to meet the men, Berti often used to go to the cafés and spend the evening chatting to other men over a Turkish coffee and a cigarette. In Albania there are not many pubs, and beer is quite expensive.

Despite the problems, some men were attracted to the church, and within five years the "Balcony Church" was too small. Since the new building had been completed, numbers had doubled from thirty to more than sixty people.

Berti began to make plans to build a new church at the back of the Victory School. Again, the church didn't have much money, so they decided to do the project in stages, first to clear the area, second to put down a floor, and finally to build the roof and the walls.

The owner, who was about to emigrate to America, allowed church members to clear the garden area and get the site ready. For the next few months, they continued to meet at the "Balcony Church", and it wasn't until April 2004 that they had enough money to pay for the floor, a job they decided had to be done by professionals. They celebrated the completion of the new floor with a special show by the school students, to which friends and family were invited. However, in the middle of the celebration, the heavens opened and they had to move hurriedly inside and complete it in the school. Now they knew they had to put a roof on as quickly as possible. To help the financial situation Berti and the board split the church and the school into two separate entities, with the church owning the site and the school paying it rent. At the same time, Hope for Albania gave them some roofing materials, which spurred them into action.

Again, members decided to build the church themselves. With help from Agim the builder, Berti the electrician and the church volunteers, including the women, mixing concrete and cement, they started building at Easter 2005. It was finished a couple of months later in June. The roof materials of the "Balcony Church", which were not suitable for the new church, were given away, so allowing Ladi to incorporate the second storey into his home.

Life became more hectic for Berti, so in November 2006, Tatjana quit her job at the court to spend more time in the church helping Berti.

On 27 July 2008, a packed Way of Peace Church celebrated its fifteenth anniversary with representatives from churches in Lushnjë, Tirana, and other Way of Peace churches, plus the Albanian Evangelical Alliance and Hope for Albania. Those who couldn't make it sent their greetings by Skype. The service gave Berti the chance to remind the congregation of all that had been achieved since the church began in 1993. "It was a joyous day," said Berti. "I told them what God had done through using ordinary people in an extraordinary way.

"The results were amazing," he continued. "We found ourselves in a beautiful building, mostly built by the hands of our own believers. We had succeeded in bringing Christianity to the people in a practical way. With the help of generous organizations, such as Hope for Albania, we had been able to help many people in the town and in the villages. We had helped the disabled, the homeless, the poor, the widows, and the orphans. We had shown everyone that God cares for the helpless and He does that through his own people, the church."

An important feature of that anniversary service was the ordination of Sokol Kertusha as the new pastor of a church in Durres, which the Way of Peace Church in Lushnjë had restarted in 2006. Every Sunday afternoon for the past year, Berti had made the two-hour round trip to Emmanuel Church, Durres, to lead the service, to preach, and to help train Sokol. During the anniversary service, Berti had prayed over him to recognize him as a full-time pastor who would carry on the work in Durres that, by tradition, was started there 2,000 years ago by the Apostle Paul himself.

Chapter 23

BEHIND EVERY DOOR THERE'S A STORY

As a trainee journalist I was told: behind every door there's a story, and if you talk to a person long enough you will find it. That is certainly true of the Way of Peace Church in Lushnjë, where probably every one of the seventy current members has a fascinating tale to tell about their journey to faith. However, there is only room here for three of them.

Servete Cani, born in 1946 in Lushnjë, was the only daughter of a very poor family. She had three brothers, but their father died when they were very young. Their father's sister, who had six older children of her own, helped look after her three nephews and a niece, while Servete's mother worked and eventually remarried. Incidentally, one of those six cousins is Vace Zela, who became one of Albania's top singers with an international reputation. To help the family finances, Servete left school at fourteen and found a job as a tailor's assistant at the factory where Ladi's father Leksi was the manager. She worked there for twenty-nine years, until it was closed in 1990 as the country moved from being a Communist to a capitalist state. Leksi told Berti that Servete, who had two sons by an arranged marriage, was a model worker. On top of that, Servete, who studied business in the evening, was so hard-working and trustworthy that he "could have given her the keys to the factory and nothing would have been touched or taken".

One of her nieces was Alma Syla, who explained the Christian message to her and invited her to the Way of Peace Church. Servete recalled, "I felt so welcomed by the church and was particularly impressed by Berti, who even though he was talking to a group of friends, saw me and came over to me." A little later, her husband Zyber, who worked for a group helping disabled people, also visited the church. Berti met him when he talked to Zyber's group after the church had been given some wheelchairs. Now they are both committed members of the church, and 63-year-old Servete is a deacon.

Bedrija Manaj, the youngest of five children, had a tough start to life. In 1943, when she was only twelve months old, her father, a farmer, was killed by a German bomb while walking along the road. Soon afterwards, her mother heard that the Germans and the Albanian collaborators, the Ballists, were closing in on her village, Sevaster, near Vlorë. She knew she couldn't escape from the village with five youngsters, so to protect Bedrija, she wrapped her in a blanket and hid her in the boughs of a nearby tree. The Germans marched straight through the village, but the Ballists stopped and explained to the villagers that they were fighting for the future of Albania – and promptly stole some of their sheep, goats, and produce. Fortunately, they didn't harm anyone. Bedrija's mother later told her that God had protected her, because she had not cried out during the three hours when the soldiers had been in the village.

Bedrija went to school in the morning and helped her mother in the afternoon, working the land. This continued until she was thirteen, when her family told her they had chosen her bridegroom. A few days later, his family came over to drink coffee with Bedrija's family and proposed a toast, wishing the couple future happiness. However, there was one person missing. They came without the future bridegroom, so Bedrija didn't meet Resul until he got out of the car on their wedding day, 28 August 1958, which was a few weeks before her sixteenth birthday. Bedrija said that for both families it was important that the boy and girl had had a good upbringing, not whether they were attracted to one another.

Compared to previous generations Bedrija was a slow starter. Her mother was married when she was twelve years old and her grandmother when she was thirteen. As both wore veils on their wedding days, their future bridegrooms had no idea what their brides looked like until they took their veils off in the bedroom after the ceremony. Bedrija said that she learnt to love her husband, Resul, who had respected her throughout her life – and they have now been happily married for fifty-one years.

After the wedding, Bedrija joined her husband in Lushnjë, where she spent fifteen years selling food at a state shop in the day and studying at night. The couple had four children and Bedrija later became an economist in the government forestry department, retiring in 1996. She started coming to church after her eldest daughter had married a Christian and a neighbour had invited Bedrija's granddaughter to Sunday school. Bedrija went along to see her granddaughter and became a church member.

She helps at the prayer meeting now. Every day she gets up at 6 a.m. and spends an hour in prayer, then two hours in Bible study, followed by another hour of prayer in the afternoon and fifteen minutes in prayer at night before she goes to sleep. She writes a daily page in her large diary of her prayer requests and folds the page over when they have been answered. She is now on volume four of her prayer diaries – and there are very few pages that haven't been folded over.

Vera Pirra, who was born in 1959 in the village of Petove, near Fier, didn't complete her schooling until she was twenty-five years old. She had had to leave school early and find a job to provide money for her parents and her two brothers and a sister. For six years she worked in a vegetable-packing factory, but then her family allowed her to go to back to school to take business studies. At the end of her first year, her three friends all failed to make it into the second year. As it was some distance away, her father, a nurse at the village clinic, wouldn't let Vera go on her own, so she had to leave.

When she visited her cousin, who worked at a flour factory in Lushnjë, he introduced her to one of his friends. A year later they were married and Vera moved into her in-laws' two-bedroom home. She soon had a son, Mikel, and when he was seven months old Vera became pregnant again. Her husband said they were so poor she would have to have an abortion. When Vera refused, he told her, "Choose me or the baby." She chose the baby. The couple divorced, and Vera returned to her village home in Petove, where her family supported her and her two children for the next two years.

In Enver Hoxha's time, the law said that a mother had the right to a home in the baby's town of birth, even if she was divorced. Vera wanted to return to Lushnjë with her two children. However, her father decided it wasn't safe for her to go on her own, so he went with her and stayed for six months, before going back to his wife in Petove. Another of Vera's cousins introduced her to Banush, a mechanic, who was widowed with a daughter and a son. She felt sorry for him and allowed him to share her house. However, as living together was frowned upon in Albania, they married in 1989 and later had a daughter, Greta.

One of the believers at the Way of Peace Church invited Greta to the Sunday school, and Vera decided to go as well. She found the church very welcoming, and as she went along to meetings, prayed, and read the Bible, she found the answers to her questions, such as "Who is God?" and "How can I find him?" Now Vera, who worked selling goods from a street stall and then as a hospital cleaner, is a deacon in the church.

Her husband, who had changed jobs from being a mechanic to working in a water irrigation firm, also started coming to church occasionally. But he was diagnosed with Parkinson's disease in 2000 and now finds it too difficult to attend. That wasn't the end of illness problems for the family: in 2006, fifteen-year-old Greta was diagnosed with scoliosis, an abnormal curvature of the spine, and was in danger of being crippled for life. Vera, accompanied by Berti and Tatjana, travelled with Greta to a specialist in Macedonia. After two years there seemed no improvement, and then they heard of a Greek professor in Tirana who would operate at a cost of 8,000 euros. The church launched an appeal and, with the help of ECM, Hope for Albania, and church members, they raised the money. Again, Berti and Tatjana went with Vera and Greta to Tirana, and ten days later they returned home with Greta after the operation. "Now Greta is walking totally normally. It really was a great answer to prayer," said Berti.

Chapter 24

LET YOUR LIGHT SHINE...

"Let your light shine before men, that they may see your good deeds and praise your Father in heaven," says Jesus in Matthew's Gospel, chapter 5 verse 16. The church takes Jesus' words and its social responsibility very seriously. Once the church was built, the congregation could concentrate on other projects, besides the Victory School, to help the community. "We want to be known by the community and for them to know who we are, so we can help them," said Berti. "We start with families, then move on to their friends, going out into the neighbourhoods, before expanding into the towns and further into the villages."

Some of these projects were more unusual, but very practical. In 2007, local youngsters thought it was great fun to use the streetlights in the road outside the church and Victory School for target practice with their catapults. The problem was that it gets dark by 4 p.m. in Lushnjë in the winter, making it unsafe for both the older and younger worshippers to come to church and school events. After discussing the problem, members decided to send Berti to the local government offices to offer them 500 dollars to buy some new streetlight bulbs with metal meshes to protect them. They accepted Berti's offer and carried out the work. "We got lots of thanks from the neighbourhood, for what was quite a small but very effective project," said Berti.

As the church grew, it became more involved in social work in Lushnjë itself. When the hospital was short of basic equipment, they helped raise money for beds, mattresses, and even surgical gloves and uniforms, through members and Hope for Albania. The charity provided gifts which church members translated into "Boxes of Joy", to give to patients when they visited the hospital. They also received from abroad shoeboxes containing sweets, pens, pencils, and shampoos, and handed them out to local children. These are now so popular that they have become an annual event.

However, it wasn't only in Lushnjë that the church began to help its local community. In the nearby villages, the church launched two of its most ambitious projects – building two homes for poor families and restoring a school. In the West, the homes where the families were living in Barbullinje and Bitaj would have been condemned as unfit for human habitation. On top of that, the children of Myzafer Cili's family in Barbullinje had never even been to school. However, although the tumbledown shacks were health risks, the families, including their young children, lived there for years, until Berti and a church team arrived. Berti contacted Hope for Albania, which provided craftsmen and materials and rebuilt the homes within six months. Now church members visit the families every month, bringing food parcels for them and other poor families. "It was great to see the joy on the families' faces when they moved into their new homes," said Berti.

One of the biggest projects the church was involved in was rebuilding the school at Gramsh, a very old and unsafe primary and secondary school, with 320 children from the ages of six to fifteen and twenty teachers.

At the same time as the church was thinking about work in the villages, officials from Hope for Albania approached Berti and said they had funds to restore a school and wanted to link up with them. Berti went to the Educational Department in Lushnjë, which gave him the names of three schools in desperate need of help, including the one at Gramsh. After praying, the church and Hope for Albania decided to help the school at Gramsh, which is seven kilometres from Lushnjë. They went to meet the chairman of the village commune, the school director, teachers, and students, who told them the school had been successful for many years. Then the building began to fall into disrepair and they couldn't afford the repairs. "We took photographs of the school, as we realized that the situation was appalling," said Berti. "The ceiling of the second floor was leaking and damaged in many places. They had abandoned the second floor, as it was dangerous to put children in the classes there. We knew that investing in the school was investing in the future of Albania," said Berti, who agreed to the project.

In the summer of 2008, while the pupils were on holiday, the charity brought in a construction company which did the majority of the restoration work. Members of Berti's church and students at the school did some of the minor jobs, including giving the whole school a major clean-up afterwards. The building work was finished in the September, in time for the new term. The villagers held a celebration and inauguration ceremony on 25 September, at which Berti explained why, as Christians, they wanted to help the school. Afterwards, much to Berti's surprise, he was called onto the stage and was presented with a certificate making him an Honorary Citizen of Gramsh. Berti added, "I was delighted and very touched with the award. It showed that the villagers were very thankful for our help with the project, which has transformed the school. It also showed everyone that we keep our promises."

He said they would like to plant a church in Gramsh one day. However, in the meantime they have continued to support the school by providing new equipment such as stoves, desks, chairs, blackboards, and sports equipment. With ECM's help, the church has supported nineteen poor families with food and clothing.

However, it wasn't just in Lushnjë and nearby villages that the church was involved. At the end of July 2009, members of the church went on a mission to Kosovo to join an international team. While the women went visiting in Peja and the nearby villages of Kyushu and Radovan, the boys played football with local teenagers, and the girls helped with painting and cleaning at the school during the day and baby-sat in the evenings so parents could attend the meetings. Bert said, "It was an enjoyable week. We built links with the church in Kosovo, and the members of our church learnt much."

Another important ministry for the church was providing wheelchairs for disabled people, because in Albania there is little state help, and many disabled people never even leave their homes. When Berti was given 200 wheelchairs by Hope for Albania in October 2007, he was left with a problem. He didn't know how to distribute that many, so he advertised on the two TV stations, offering them free to families who called him. As they came to the church, Berti gave them the wheelchairs and then offered them free English and computer courses at the Victory School as well. After nine students completed the course seven months later, they held a big award ceremony in the church to which town officials, including the director of the employment office, as well as friends and family, came. "One of the aims was to give disabled people a chance to integrate into our society," said Berti. "By learning to use a computer and to speak English they have a better opportunity to find work, which is very hard in Albania."

To help disabled people further, Alma, who taught at a state school in the morning and at the Victory School in the afternoon, linked up with one of the town schools. "We wanted to make children aware that these people are part of society, even though they have been hidden away for years and years," she added. "They also need our love, our care, and our support."

Many had been impressed by the church's efforts over the years, including Dr Janet Goodall and Mervyn Kirkpatrick, a social worker with the Causeway Trust in Northern Ireland. Dr Goodall said, "Few people bothered about disabled people in Albania. So when Berti and his church became involved, it was a huge step forward in that country and showed the caring side of the pastor and the church."

In July 2005, Mervyn had joined an ECM team visiting Lushnjë and was so moved that he decided to spend part of his retirement helping them. "Disability is not something that is highlighted in Albanian society, nor are there adequate facilities for families caring for disabled relatives," he said after his visit. "During our time preparing for the church project, we were able to locate in the country only one facility for mental health, one school for children with learning disabilities, and one facility for physical disabilities."

Mervyn decided to launch a day care centre in partnership with the church, and in June 2008 they began a pilot two-week project. Berti, whose church had been preparing for this event for a year, said, "We aimed to help people with mental and physical disabilities, to show them Christ's love, as well as to awake in the patients and their family members the hope of change in their way of living."

The team consisted of seven individuals from various churches in Northern Ireland, including a physiotherapist, two occupational therapists, a social worker, a music therapist, and two youth workers. Fourteen members of the Lushnjë church were trained to work alongside the Irish team. Along with the local church volunteers, the team set up a day care facility in the church for the seventeen children and adults. The programme, called Way of Hope, consisted of arts and crafts, sports and games, music, and refreshments, and ended with massage and relaxation. "Throughout our time with the young people and their carers we could see an improvement in their confidence and social skills," said Mervyn. "Many of them learned new skills and tried new things, such as music, games and crafts."

He said the carers were challenged by the project as they saw how their children developed in such a short time, and how they interacted with the other young people and the adults. Berti added, "The families of the patients were also hugely impacted by the project. Experiencing our love, acceptance, care, and friendliness, the parents saw how their children played with others, and it was wonderful to hear them worship God and being open to follow the way of their hope, Jesus Christ."

Some of the families started attending church because they had seen how loved and accepted their children were. Two people who really enjoyed the project were Blerim and Taulant. Blerim is in his early twenties and has epileptic fits three or four times a day. He was not accepted at school, so had to stay at home with only his family for company and was not used to socializing. Mervyn said, "During his two weeks at the centre he had no epileptic seizures and took part in everything, excelling in sports and games. We watched as Blerim progressed into a confident young man who did not rely on his father's help during his time with us. It was wonderful to see how proud his parents were to see him interact with others and enjoying himself."

Taulant, who is in his late teens, has cerebral palsy and cannot speak. "Yet," said Mervyn, "he took part in everything, and the smile on his face said it all." This was the first time Tauland had been able to go out of his house and walk around in the community with his family, as he was often left in his room on his own to watch TV. Mervyn added, "His sister found it especially difficult to have a brother with cerebral palsy and was never seen outside the house with him. Over the two weeks we watched as Taulant and his family had the time of their lives at the centre, with his sister coming along daily and enjoying spending time with her brother."

Another of those at the club was fifty-year-old Marika, who again had left her home for the first time in her life to come to the day care project. The team were delighted by her enthusiasm and excitement as she threw herself into everything going on.

The event finished with a ceremony where each member was presented with a certificate of achievement. Before they set off back home, they went to the park in Lushnjë, where they were treated to an orange juice and an ice cream. Although this is a common event in the West, it was very unusual then in Albania.

But one hour later, after Marika had arrived home, her heart stopped and she died. Berti said, "Marika's sister told me she had gone back so happy and so excited by all that had happened during the fortnight." A few days later Berti, who with Mervyn oversaw the funeral, which was attended by the helpers, added, "There was not a dry eye in the church that day."

Chapter 25

BERTI PUTS ON HIS RADIO HEADPHONES AGAIN

Because Berti had discovered Christianity through the radio, he was always keen that Albanians should have that opportunity as well.

In 2003, Trans World Radio had helped an Albanian Christian organization, Waves of the Gospel, to set up Radio 7 in Tirana to provide programmes to beam throughout their country. Two years later Berti was delighted to be invited to join the radio board as chairman, along with another pastor, a representative from Trans World Radio, two representatives from Radio 7, and two from Waves of the Gospel. Because there are so many other stations providing news, Radio 7 is 90 per cent Christian programmes and 10 per cent news.

One person who was particularly delighted by this was Peter Harrison, who had spent twenty-three years producing the tapes, and later using computer technology, to send Sali Rahmani's and Rifat Buzuku's recorded messages via Trans World Radio into Albania. He said, "I always thought this work could be done by Albanian Christians and I was delighted when I was able to pass it on."

Monday is Berti's only day off. But he spends many of his rest days on a three-hour round trip to Radio 7 at Prush, Tirana, to record his two programmes – *Words of Hope*, a twenty-minute programme which covers different Christian topics and goes out five days a week, and a three-minute devotional thought for the day, which is transmitted daily. "Even though I am very busy, I am really glad God has allowed me to provide this special service," said Berti. He knows people are listening, because he bumps into friends who comment on the programmes, and listeners send him letters.

Already the programmes are transmitted to most of Albania, but the station is planning to improve its transmission. "I am so excited to receive the letters and my heart is full of joy about what is happening," said Berti. "God is using me on the radio in the same way He brought the gospel to me through the radio all those years ago."

Thirty years ago at the army base, he had to put on his radio headphones and listen secretly to the Christian programmes. Today, on most Mondays Berti puts on his radio headphones and openly broadcasts the Christian message to his fellow Albanians, who for most of their life had been told there is no God. It is on the same frequency the Enver Hoxha regime had used to put out its atheistic propaganda to its people and its neighbours. What a delicious irony.

THE FINAL THOUGHTS HAVE TO GO TO BERTI:

First, I want to thank God for entering my life and being present ever since. He has reached me, someone who had never thought much about God. He has taken me from darkness and brought me to light.

I am grateful to many people who have helped me to know God and to serve him.

I want to thank especially Stephen Bell, who has always been with me in my ministry.

I thank Gani Smolica, whom God used at a turning point in my life in Christ.

I thank all the brothers and sisters of ECM, and especially Arthur Prescott, who has been very patient with me.

Thank you to Douglas Livingston, who gave me the vision for Victory School.

Especially, I am very thankful to Charles Ball, Donna Rosales, and others from Calvary Church who have blessed our church with their gifts of evangelism.

Thank you to Alma, Vera, Servete, and Bedrije, who have ministered in the Victory School and the Way of Peace Church untiringly.

Thank you to Lenci and Alta Mene, a young couple with a great vision for the Albanian church, who have given me great support and encouragement to continue boldly in building the church and who have helped me have a clear vision for the Victory School, to use it in God's service.

In addition, I want to thank the Hope for Albania foundation, especially Pier and Anette, who have made it possible for us to have a building to meet in and who have enabled our church to help people in need with practical aid.

These people are not in the book, but I would like to thank:

Ron Anderson of ECM, who has been very patient with me.

Jurgen Sachs, who has had a great influence in my life and has been a wise teacher.

Steve Valkenburg, who has been a great supporter in the church's community projects.

Janet King, who has become a great encouragement for the Victory School in its ministry;

Co-workers Alfred Jani and Doke Dimashi, who have given much for the Way of Peace Church and for Victory School, but are now with the Lord.

Finally, I am thankful to my loving wife Tatjana, who has been by my side in good and bad moments in our life and who has been very patient with me during all these years.

I also want to thank author John Butterworth, who has worked tirelessly for many months in putting together this book. I know the project has helped him continue on his spiritual journey.

My story has been His story as God has used so many different people from all over the world, some of whom I have never met, as I have journeyed from being Captain Dosti to becoming Pastor Dosti. At the same time, I believe that God has been with the country of Albania on its journey from isolated dictatorship to open democracy. Enver Hoxha claimed in 1967 that God did not exist, but I believe God has proved that he does exist, and thousands of Albanian Christians will testify to that.

And to the readers of this book, what about your journey through life? I pray that your story might not be a mere collection of haphazard meetings, but rather that through people in the past, present and future you might meet the living God and my Saviour.

POSTSCRIPT:

WHAT ON EARTH HAPPENED TO...?

I find it fascinating to follow what happened to the people mentioned in the Gospels through to the Acts of the Apostles and the rest of the New Testament. Even today, after reading a book or seeing a play, I always want to know what became of the characters and to tie up the loose ends.

If, like me, you want to know what became of the personalities in modern Albania's "Book of Acts", here is what happened to them. I have listed the people in alphabetical order.

Alma Syla: She is a deacon and a leading member of the Way of Peace Church in Lushnjë and the senior teacher at the Victory School. Married to Drini, she has two daughters, Sabrina and Kaltrina.

Andre: He was one of the guides whom Stephen Bell met on his first visit to Albania. He became a Christian and now helps to translate messages for the *Words of Hope* programme at Radio 7 in Tirana.

Antoneta: Berti's mother moved to Greece with her son after her second husband died, but she moved back to Korçë in 2006.

Arthur Prescott: He was sent out by ECM to help in the 1999 refugee crisis. He is living near Solihull, but he still goes to Albania and Kosovo regularly. His church organized a "Raise the Roof" project, filling a lorry with shoeboxes and other goods and driving it out to Kosovo. For a time he was acting field leader, helping and encouraging Albanian and Kosovan church leaders, including Berti and Gani.

Barbara Howarth (née Jamieson): She was the ECM worker in Vienna who invited Sali Rahmani to church and the start of his Christian journey. Barbara returned to England in the late 1970s, and in 1980 she married Jim Howarth, a widower and an ECM missionary in France. Jim then became pastor of Harbourside Evangelical Church in Bridlington until he died in 2003. Barbara is now retired, but still helps at the Harbourside Church.

Bledi: He was the twelve-year-old boy who came to the first meeting of the Patos church at which there were also twenty-five women. Bledi went to Italy, but has now returned to Patos, where he is an active member of the church.

Canon Jack and Elsie Bell: Stephen's parents who supported his work in Albania. Jack was vicar of Mosley Common for twenty years until he retired in 1989. He and Elsie live in Kendal in the Lake District.

David Clark: He accompanied Sali and other ECM supporters on a day trip to Albania from Corfu. After serving with ECM for twenty years in various leadership roles, latterly as International director, David retired in 2004. His last project was to write a brief history of the mission, *Sharing Christ's Love in Europe*. This formed part of the centenary celebrations of ECM in 2004. He now lives in Halesowen, near Birmingham, and continues to be involved in a preaching and teaching ministry, as well as enjoying more time with family and grandchildren.

Dosti family: Berti and Tatjana continue to live in Lushnjë, where Berti still runs the Way of Peace Church and the Victory School. In 2008, Berti was also appointed ECM Field Leader for Albania and Kosovo.

Berti and Tatjana's daughter Alta and her husband Lenci are in Holland, where Lenci is studying for a Masters degree in evangelical theology, while Berti and Tatjana's son Dorian is taking a business studies degree at a university in Tirana.

Doug Groth: He accompanied Stephen Bell on a flying visit to Prishtina, Kosovo. Doug and his wife Lila are still working for ECM, church-planting in Poland.

Dr Leonard Loose: He marked Berti's Soon Bible correspondence course and papers from students all over the world for twenty-five years, until he died on 27 March 2007 at the age of ninety-six.

ECM: The missionary society, which moved to Northampton in 1985, has 130 missionaries from twenty different nationalities working all over Europe. ECM can be contacted at 50 Billing Road, Northampton NN1 5DH, England, by phone on 01604 621092, or by email at ecm.gb@ecmi.org. Its website is www.ecmbritain.org.

Enver Hoxha's pyramid: Hoxha's daughter Primavera designed the tribute to her father, which opened in 1988 as a museum. However, within three years it was closed, and all the exhibits were removed. It became briefly a disco before being turned into the Albanian International Cultural Centre. The pyramid building is still there in the centre of Tirana.

Esmeralda: She wrote one of the first letters from Albania to ECM via Trans World Radio. She went to study law at a Polish university and is now living in Tirana, but is unemployed and does not go to church. "However," she said, "I carry the Trans World Radio Bible with me all the time and read it regularly. When I went to Poland I put it in my luggage and it was a source of great comfort to me." Her parents, Llambi and Parashqevi, still live in Lushnjë, while Esmeralda's sister Senola, who studied chemistry, lives in Tirana with her husband, who is a businessman, and their two sons.

Evis: She interpreted for Dr Janet Goodall in Albania and in England when "Lucy" came over for a number of operations. Evis went to study at Harvard University in America, where she read law and met a German professor of modern history who was there on a short course from Buffalo. They are married, have two young boys, and live in America.

Gani and Adile Smolica: Gani met Stephen Bell at Prishtina University, where they became friends. The Smolicas joined Stephen in Albania 1993 and stayed there until June 2000, when they left to work for ECM in Peja, Kosovo.

Genci: He taught Berti Italian and helped translate his Italian correspondence course. He lives in Kemishtaj, a village near Lushnjë, with his daughter. He got divorced, although he has now met someone else. Genci, who is from an Orthodox background, rediscovered a living faith in 2005. He is employed by Berti and teaches Italian to twenty pupils at the Victory School in the afternoon. In the morning, he teaches Italian at a private school. He attends a Mennonite Church in Lushnjë.

Gëzim, Lida, and Xhovi: The three were converted at a Vlorë summer camp. They wanted Stephen to start churches in their home towns of Berat and Fier, which he did. Gëzim, having returned from Bible school in Germany, later helped start a church in Seman, near Fier. He is still involved in the church there.

Lida, who was a nurse at an army hospital, married Romeo, from Korçë, who was a member of the Albanian Symphony Orchestra and who translated English Bible commentaries into Albanian. They are involved in a church in Tirana.

Xhovi is married with two children.

Iliri: Berti's brother is living in Lezhe after retiring from the police. He is now a caretaker at a private firm, while his wife is a doctor. They have a son, Ildi, who is doing a business studies degree at a university in Tirana. He shares a flat with Berti's son Dorian.

Ismet, Violeta, and Klodian: Stephen stayed with Ismet, Violeta, and their son Klodian when he first went to live in Albania. They adopted Stephen as their "son", and Ismet went to Stephen and Tabita's wedding. Klodian became an Orthodox priest for a while. He is now married with two children. Ismet's wife Violeta died in March 2010.

Jack Murray: He was ECM's International director and the first chairman of the Albanian Encouragement Project. When he retired from ECM, Jack and his wife Martha went to California, where he was mission pastor of a church. Now Jack, who lives near Sacramento, does some counselling work and keeps in touch by email with around eighty-five retired ECM workers. His wife Martha died in October 2009.

Janet Goodall: The paediatrician who went out to Albania with Sali Rahmani and Ron Newby is now retired and lives in North Staffordshire, but still supports Albania and Albanians working in England.

Kashmiri: Berti's friend translated one of his correspondence courses and was the interpreter at the first church service in Lushnjë. He is married with a son and lives in Tirana, but works in an office in Lushnjë translating documents in Albanian, Serbian, English, German, and Italian for customers.

Kristaq: An officer with Berti in the Rapid Defence Force, he translated replies from Trans World Radio for him. An Italian-speaker from an Orthodox background, he now lives in a village outside Lushnjë. Berti has seen him only once recently, when Kristaq asked him for a job, but unfortunately Berti was unable to help.

Ladi: He is Berti's lifelong friend and business partner in the kiosk in Lushnjë, which they set up in 1992. Ladi now works in a car accessories kiosk in Lushnjë. He still lives in the same house where Berti and his team built the church on the first floor. He has added another floor, where he now lives. There are four shops on the ground floor, which Ladi rents out, and he also rents out the second floor to a missionary. Ladi's parents Leksi and Liri, who are both retired now, still live next door.

"Lucy": She is the girl Dr Janet Goodall brought to England for medical help. She has made excellent progress and is now studying at a university in Tirana.

Margaret Willan: She went on the first ever holiday to Albania with Barbara Jamieson in 1975. She continued working for ECM in Munich and then New Zealand until she retired in 2006. She is now living in Harrogate and is involved with organizing English camps in Hungary.

Mervyn Kirkpatrick: He was the Northern Ireland social worker who came to help disabled people in Lushnjë. He died in 2009. However, his work lives on, with a party from Northern Ireland going out to run another joint project with Berti's church to help disabled people.

Myzafer Cili family: The Lushnjë church and Hope for Albania helped this family by rebuilding their derelict home. As both parents, their son, and a daughter are all disabled, they have difficulty getting to church. They come occasionally when Berti picks them up.

Peter and Susi Harrison: Peter was the radio technician who had helped prepare Sali Rahmani's radio messages for Trans World Radio to beam into Albania. He did that job for twenty-three years from 1981 until 2004, when he handed the work over to Berti and the Albanian Christians. From 2004, Peter and Susi continued working for ECM, but they were seconded to a Swiss mission to help at a Christian bookshop in Klagenfurt, in southern Austria, near the Slovenian border. Although Peter is now officially at retirement age, he is still working there, as well as doing some preaching and visitation work. They have two daughters, a son, and six grandchildren.

Petro: He was the son of a language professor at Tirana University with whom Ron Newby, Dr Janet Goodall, and Sali Rahmani stayed when they went to Albania in September 1991. Petro later went to Russia to join his mother's family.

Phil Butterworth: Stephen Bell still sees his friend from youth club days. Phil is living in Leigh, where he is a driving instructor and a lay leader in the Independent Methodist Church. He is married, with three children.

Rifat Buzuku: He was the Kosovan who worked with ECM in the Vienna office, helping provide radio messages for Trans World Radio. After nearly eighteen years with ECM he left in 2004 and is now an IT manager in Austria. He has two children and still attends church.

Ron Newby: He founded the charity Global Care in 1999 and went out to Albania with Dr Janet Goodall and Sali Rahmani in September 1991. In 1999, Ron received an MBE for his work with vulnerable children worldwide. Ron died in 2008. Today, Global Care continues to support needy children and young people in more than forty projects worldwide.

Sadete: The postwoman who delivered to the Lushnjë kiosk the Trans World Radio/ECM replies to Berti's letters. She lost her job in 1995 shortly before the Lushnjë post office was privatized. Later, she met a believer from Berti's church, became a regular there, and was baptized in 2003. Her husband is a believer as well. They have two boys and now go to another church in Lushnjë.

Sali Rahmani: Sali was the radio presenter, operator, and producer Berti listened to in secret. Sali left ECM in 1997. He is now living in Northamptonshire, where he helps and preaches at five rural churches and works as a translator and an interpreter for the NHS and the police. He is editing and writing Bible study courses in Albanian with Manna Publications and helping Word for the World in Bible translating. Sali is also involved with the Holy Cross churches in Malawi. Sali remarried a Ukrainian Christian, Olena, in 2005 and they have a foster son, Arron.

Shau Ping: He was Stephen's Chinese friend in Prishtina. He became an Austrian citizen.

Stephen and Tabita Bell: They played a major part in the life of Berti and the Albanian church. The couple, who now have three children, Sheona, Joshua, and Benjamin, left Albania in 2000 to carry on with ECM in Croatia, planting churches in Zagreb.

Stephen Etches: He translated both the New Testament and the Bible into modern Albanian. His speciality was languages and he later taught extensively at a seminary in Yugoslavia before returning to England. He now lives in Kent.

Stuart Rowell: He was the ECM Eastern European director who worked with Berti, and as a construction engineer advised him on building the "Balcony Church." Stuart works part time for ECM Ireland and travels regularly to Eastern Europe to help missionaries and national pastors.

Tom Lewis: He was ECM's Eastern European director who went to bring Sali Rahmani and Peter Harrison home after Sali had been interrogated in Yugoslavia. Tom left ECM in 1990 to work with Biblical Education by Extension (BEE World), a ministry he helped found in 1979 while working with ECM in Vienna. BEE provides advanced Bible training to pastors in restricted access areas of the world. As BEE UK director, Tom has helped develop the work in

China and has been responsible for BEE's ministry in Vietnam for the last fifteen years and providing Bible courses over the internet. Tom and his wife Doreen have three sons and two granddaughters.

Trans World Radio: TWR works in more than 200 languages and dialects covering 160 countries. In the UK, TWR broadcasts quality, speech-led Christian radio nationally via satellite, the internet, and (at selected times) on short and medium wave. In the north west of England broadcasts are also available on DAB digital radio. TWR can be contacted at PO Box 606, Altrincham, WA14 2YS, by phone on 0161 923 0270, by email at info@twr.org.uk or via the website www.twt.org.uk.

Tunnels of Albania: After Enver Hoxha's death, there was no need for the labyrinth of tunnels built for the population in the event of a military attack. Some did go to ruin, but many residents bought the tunnels underneath their homes to use as a wine cellar or storeroom, while others used them to grow mushrooms or breed turkeys and geese. Even the homeless found them a useful place to stay in overnight. Others are used to store goods and animals. One enterprising family has added a gate and turned the pillbox on their land into a duck house.

Veria: He was the first letter writer from Albania to Trans World Radio. Now an elderly man, he is living in Fier, but still attends church.

Victory School: The school founded by the church in Lushnjë continues to grow and in early 2010 had a record 526 pupils with fifteen English teachers and four support staff, plus two Italian classes, four computing classes, and two sewing lessons every week. They have an ambitious scheme to expand, including a plan to open a kindergarten.

REFERENCES

Chapter 1

1 Jim Forest, *The Resurrection of the Church in Albania. Voices of Orthodox Christians*, WCC Publications.
2 John R. W. Stott, *The Message of Acts*, The Bible Speaks Today, IVP, page 316.

Chapter 2

1 James Pettifer, *Blue Guide: Albania and Kosovo*.
2 ibid.
3 ibid.

Chapter 3

1 James Pettifer, *Blue Guide: Albania and Kosovo*.
2 ibid.

Chapter 4

1 James Pettifer, *Blue Guide: Albania and Kosovo*.
2 ibid.

Chapter 6

1 David Clark (ed.), *Sharing Christ's Love in Europe*, ECM International, 2004.

Chapter 9

1 Dr Paul E. Freed, *Towers to Eternity*, Trans World Radio.

Chapter 10

1 James Pettifer, *Blue Guide: Albania and Kosovo*.

Chapter 12

1 Bill Hamilton, *Albania – Who Cares?* Autumn House.

Chapter 13

1 *Albania's Empty-Handed Freedom*, European Christian Mission.
2 James Pettifer, *Blue Guide: Albania and Kosovo*.

Chapter 15

1 John Quanrud, *A Sacred Task*, Authentic Lifestyle.

Chapter 21

1 James Pettifer, *Blue Guide: Albania and Kosovo*.
2 John Quanrud, *A Sacred Task*, Authentic Lifestyle.
3 Bill Hamilton, *Albania – Who Cares?* Autumn House.

OTHER BOOKS FROM MONARCH:

Out of the Black Shadows
Anne Coomes

ISBN 978 1 85424 772 8
£8.99

Life Lessons From a Horse Whisperer
Dr Lew Sterrett with Bob Smietana

ISBN 978 1 85424 918 0
£7.99

For more information please go to **www.lionhudson.com**